# EMOTION and ART:

## Mastering the Artist's Path

----------

# JOHN RUSKAN

R. Wyler & Co., New York

EMOTION AND ART: Mastering the Artist's Path

by JOHN RUSKAN

Copyright © 2012 John Ruskan

ISBN: 978-0-9629295-4-0

R. Wyler & Co.

NY NY 10011

Contact email: rwylerpub@gmail.com

dedicated to artists everywhere

# contents

## part 3: Feelings About Making Art

# The Evolution of Consciousness

Becoming an artist is something that happens when you're not looking. At some point, you realize that you have values, interests, and goals different from what might be called the materialistic orientation. You don't particularly care that you live in less than glamorous surroundings. On the contrary, you create a sense of soulfulness wherever you are. You don't like spending a large portion of your time working only to make money. You would rather work less and play creatively more. In other words, you are not of the ordinary, you are different from the mainstream. You are on a journey, and whether you know it or not, it's the journey of consciousness evolution.

You may make a practice of expressing yourself - your feelings or ideas - in some kind of media that could be called art. Or, you might not yet be at the point, or need, of concretizing inner abstractions. The important thing is that you've entered a phase of life marked by a radical shifting of values. What's important now is not what you *have* on the outside, but what you *feel* on the inside. Are you happy with yourself? Are you managing inner feelings satisfactorily? Are you growing on all levels, emotionally, intellectually, and creatively? Are you continually finding new parts of yourself, new abilities that keep you fascinated? This spontaneous, inner development can be thought of as consciousness evolution, and could be said to be a central purpose of life.

What might be most helpful for you is a guide that would explain the inner path upon which you have embarked, from the artistic viewpoint, and hopefully offer some pertinent information about how to navigate it successfully. This is what this book attempts to do.

As we survey the art that is being produced at this moment in history, we find an incredibly diverse assortment of creative offerings. This is to be regarded as a great boon. The diversity in itself distinguishes this period from previous periods. We see art that has an apparent connection to inner personal feelings, and art that does not have such an obvious link. Regrettably, from the viewpoint of this book, much of today's art may be said to fall into this second category, although it is, of course, impossible to create any composition or object that is not a reflection of the inner on some level. But much of today's art does appear to be relatively impersonal, with an absence of emphasis on feeling.

To a certain extent, the conditions under which art is made today, by artists who are not just dabbling, can contribute to this impersonality in art. Artists are under tremendous pressures. We need to support ourselves financially, and find time to do our art. Then we need to market the art. These three areas alone demand more time than we have available. We can easily become stressed out and competitive because the marketplace is competitive. We start to evaluate our art from the standpoint of its commercial viability - will it stand out, is it good enough? All this tends to keep us producing a product and striving after success. Whenever the emphasis is on results, not only in the art field, feelings tend to get put aside, because they don't matter. The foundation of modern, competitive, materialistic society is feeling-repressed goal-orientation, and artists too can easily fall into this aggressive, insensitive mindset.

What this present book suggests, however, is that art can be much more than just a vehicle for the achievement of the ego. Art can be primarily a journey to the Self, a way inward towards self-understanding, balance, growth, and true happiness, and it can be one of the most powerful routes. The journey starts when you include a personal feeling component in the art you are making, and I believe this can be done in any genre, any style. You have already begun this journey - this journey of consciousness evolution - just by becoming interested in the art path. You may only need to deepen your understanding of the principles involved to maximize your art experience.

This present work is a project near and dear to my heart, something I have yearned to complete for a long time. It follows my first book, *Emotional Clearing*. It was natural for me to combine my two major interests - psychology and art - into a book that would clarify how they can complement each other, since they have become inextricably intertwined in my own personal practice. This book is not a pep talk to get you doing art. It certainly does not offer advice on technique in any particular media. Rather, it addresses the inner problems that serious artists of all disciplines encounter in their work.

I believe I have not just revisited themes previously explored in the literature of art or art therapy, but that I have broken some new ground, particularly in the understanding of the artistic manic-depressive syndrome, the three stages of making art, and how the main benefit of art for consciousness transformation and healing comes about through the projection and recognition of the suppressed self in the art as it is being created, rendering the process of art-making inspirational, transcendent, and glorious.

Throughout the book I have referred to classic artists of the twentieth century rather than current artists who might exemplify the points I am making. I have done this because we understand these older artists and their work well. Moreover, to be honest, these are the artists I know. I would have a hard time trying to find current artists, in any genre, well-known and documented enough today to illustrate the discussion.

Only time will tell if classic artists will emerge from this current decade, the first of the twenty-first century. Of course, we would expect that they will, but there is also room for doubt. Will today's art have long-term impact similar to the art of previous times? Has the quality of art slipped? Sometimes, from certain points of view it appears so, and that we are in a dark period, even with the abundance of art at our fingertips.

But to whatever extent today's art may be lacking, I would suggest that a primary reason is the absence of personal feeling content. One of the highest attributes of art lies in its ability to both contain feelings and to be an important means of unearthing these feelings from the subconscious, whether art is engaged as an observer or as a creator. This is a primary factor that gives personal and lasting value to art, and enables it to be a vital force not only for culture and communication, but for the evolution of consciousness.

I wish you well on your journey.

John Ruskan       New York 2011

# part one

Art As A Pathway To Feeling

# 1

# What Is Art?

*Right-brain presence as the basis for art;*
*Understanding left and right brain;*
*What is art? John's story*

It's 1981, New York City. I've just been to my first performance of Squat Theater. Squat Theater is a group of about fifteen Hungarian performers, including some children. They have recently arrived in the US and have rented a storefront on West 23rd Street in Chelsea, around the corner from my loft on 22nd Street.

The artistic climate in New York at this time is vibrant, possibly more than it's ever been or will be. A new art esthetic known as *postmodern* is emerging. Soho is underway, and not yet destroyed. The East Village is starting to happen, with tons of small galleries opening there, displaying the art of young unknown artists – *East Village Art*, it is to be called. A kind of rock music called *New Wave* is breaking, incorporating precepts that are revolutionary in the ongoing evolution of pop music. *Experimental* and *avant-garde* are the norm but the overriding artistic buzz-word is *multimedia* – the combining of all art forms into one: drama, music, painting, film, sculpture, dance, poetry.

There are several key ensembles in town that have adopted this model and are delivering unprecedented creative work: Meredith Monk, the Wooster St. Performance Group, Richard Foreman, Laurie Anderson, Mabou Mines, and Squat Theater, along with a multitude of other less prominent theater, music, and dance groups. Affiliated with them are newcomers such as Philip Glass and Spaulding Gray.

## presence

Squat Theater is presenting *Pig Child Fire,* which will win an Obie, a landmark achievement for an experimental, off, off Broadway company. I am there for one of the first performances; I will go back to see it three more times. The production leaves me stunned. It transcends theater and becomes a mystical experience of *presence*; presence that begins in the theater, but is taken beyond the *borders* of the theater and with me as I leave.

*Pig Child Fire* consists of about six unrelated vignettes, all without dialogue – which is convenient since none of the cast speaks English – and apparently, without plot. Just scenes. The scenes have some orchestrated movement, but most are largely spontaneous, with no planned direction. Still, I would not call it improvisational. Improvisation, at least in the theater, implies that some plot is being generated as a piece unfolds. This is not the case, since no plot ever develops.

One of the unique elements of the "performance" is the setting: a storefront, on street level. The seats for the audience are placed at the back of the space, ramping upwards towards the ceiling as they go farther back, facing the front of the store, where there is the stage area, and behind that a large, floor to ceiling plate glass window looking out onto the sidewalk. A passerby on 23rd Street – a major, busy street – can look into the undraped window as the performance is underway and see everything that happens.

However, the lighting in the theater and the glare from looking in through the window is such that it is not easy to discern the audience in darkness behind the stage, especially in the evening, when the performances are given. People walking by then see the performance through the glass, stop to watch it and interact with it without particularly knowing they are being watched by the audience, not even necessarily realizing a performance is in progress. The interaction of the people on the street with the performance is unbelievable. People stand looking in, completely unselfconsciously, obviously mesmerized, elated, horrified, amused or incensed. Incognito, members of the cast mingle with the crowd outside, interacting in both subtle and provocative ways, sometimes apparently asking for money or sex, sometimes almost to the point of getting punched or slapped.

One of the objectives of the theater (shared by other stage companies at this time) is the unification of art and reality, the breaking of the artificial barrier between art and audience. This is achieved in a completely unique way, not with the audience who is aware of the trick, but with the unsuspecting crowd outside, who becomes a spontaneous part of the performance. The cast members on the street further the fusion as they pass between the two worlds.

The scenes of the performance range from pastoral to surreal, with even the gentle pastoral settings becoming bizarre in contrast. For example, the breakfast scene. This is simply a mother having breakfast with three children, ages 5 to 10. There is nothing else to the scene, which goes on for perhaps fifteen minutes – it is simply an exercise in being present: pouring orange juice into glasses, cereal and milk into bowls, with the kids absolutely in the moment, unaware of any audience, and the mother radiating peacefulness, talking to them in their native language.

Once you understand that nothing is going to happen in the scene, your mind goes on hold. Expectation is suspended, and as a viewer, you come into the moment also – shatteringly. Shattered is the sense of looking forward, of needing something to happen to take you out of where you are; shattered is the neurotic ego that wants, wants, wants. It's just you, the kids, the mother, the faces on the other side of the glass (also entranced), with no thought of the future. The sense of presence is breathtaking.

Other scenes are more stirring and some violent, displaying presence in turmoil. After five minutes of animated disagreement between two players, one of them places his arm on a wooden table, reaches for an ax, and chops off his hand at the wrist, blood gushing. It's not for several minutes that the audience realizes the arm is fake.

At times, a video camera on the street is capturing images and relaying them back to a monitor inside for the audience to see. Some of these images are beyond the line of sight of the audience looking through the window, some just present a simultaneous, alternative view of what the audience can already see. In one segment, a female player stands on a box outside on the sidewalk with her back to the window, sensitively and with feeling reading a long poem in her native language to the outside crowd. She's wearing an ankle length white skirt that is puffed out by hoops sewn into the fabric. Under the skirt, built into the box, is a bright white light that shines upwards between her legs, illuminating the entire skirt, making her appear somewhat angelic. What the audience on the street does not know is that next to the light under the skirt is a video camera, aimed directly at the young woman's crotch, not covered by any underwear, the image of which is displayed on the monitor to the inside audience. Apparently, she is reading an erotic poem, and we are enabled to perceive subtle physiological changes occurring as she becomes stimulated by the poetry.

This scene could easily degenerate into a sensationalistic, vulgar display, but the point is that it does not. The sensitivity of the reading, the trust of the performer in the outside crowd and the inside audience, the abandonment, the absolute sense of presence, the feeling that something mystical is happening, take precedence over any hint of embarrassment.

In another segment, a jeep with players pulls up on the sidewalk and creates a commotion. The players start arguing and fighting with each other and then move inside to continue their brawl. In their rage, they throw objects at a stuffed mannequin that has been hanging during the entire performance – about an hour – from the ceiling in a corner of the stage. At once, the mannequin comes alive and starts to move, arms and legs thrashing wildly in response to being attacked, and then goes limp again. There has been a person motionless inside the whole time – an impressive demonstration of control. Life and stage-set, real and fake, reality and fantasy are again blended to make one. The effect is shocking and startling.

During much of the play, there's taped raw rock music creating a sense of urgency and wildness that is balanced by the softness and sensitivity of the players. But what comes across most is the timelessness, of moving into the present, that this performance could never work unless it was formed around an exquisitely conscious sense of presence. Being present, in the moment, with no thought of being anywhere else, with total acceptance of whatever happens on the street, where anything could happen and does; being present to the simple moment and transforming it into mystical experience. This is what the mystical experience is.

Art takes place in the present. After we have learned the tools of our trade, whether it's the chords, the steps, the brush technique, or how to deliver lines, we allow those tools to be shaped by the present, by our experience of the present, in the present, particularly allowing for the inclusion of *feeling*. This sense of the present is especially important when we choose to incorporate art in a conscious program of personal growth.

## left and right

How are we to understand more fully and develop this all-important quality of presence? We address this concern throughout the book, but to start with, we might look at how presence relates to the concept of left and right-brain. Even though the idea of left and right-brain is well-known today, it is important for us to discuss it to make sure we have a common understanding, since our basic approach to art is founded on these concepts.

Left and right-brain refer to the two major modes available to us for the perception, reaction, and interaction with the world around us, each mode ostensibly based in one of the hemispheres of the brain. We can consciously choose the mode in which we wish to operate, and shift between them as circumstances or our inclinations dictate. Our goal is to develop and find a balance for the two modes, and to make sure neither is atrophied or overwhelms the other.

The left-brain mode refers to behavior associated with the masculine archetype – aggressive, willful, rational, productive; and the right-brain mode with the feminine archetype – supportive, accepting, subjective, nurturing. The left-brain is concerned with thinking, reasoning, and logic – the movement of thought through time, and creates our perception of the linear, time-bound universe, where events happen sequentially, in order. The right-brain is associated with feelings, emotions, and intuition, and is the seat of mystical consciousness, of going beyond time, being in the moment, of being somehow more soulful, and perhaps most importantly, being *present*. Thus, when we align ourselves with the right-brain, deliberately awakening attributes of the right-brain, we automatically start to come into the present.

You can easily see the difference between the two modes by just being aware of your state of mind. In the left-brain, you are usually evaluating, planning, and striving after some presumed desirable outcome. This goal-orientation leaves you with an agenda. You tend to reject anything that does not fit with it, including circumstances, people, and even your feelings. Over a period of time, such judgmentalism can have drastic consequences on your well-being. It's easy to end up frustrated and unfulfilled when functioning primarily in the left-brain, and not even understand why.

When you are in the right-brain, your sense of being is notably different. First, you feel more in the body, and not in the head because the right-brain feeling function is connected to the body; feelings occur in the body. Those who are unfamiliar with this sensation because they have never been out of the head will have difficulty comprehending what I'm talking about. Being in the body connects you to the earth, because your body is of the earth; and to a greater sense of oneness and a marked reduction of the inherent isolation of the left-brain.

In the right-brain there's less reliance on reasoning, of trying to think your way through everything. A more intuitive certainty takes over. Gone is the subtle rejection of feelings that accompanies the thinking orientation. You seem to be floating, perhaps even out in space. You no longer need to struggle to make things turn out well; it seems easy to trust. Above all, there's a gentle sense of being in the moment – just being here now; being present; not needing to strive to get anywhere. You begin to access the mystical realms of the soul – the place where art originates.

Being in the right-brain does not mean all negative feelings automatically evaporate. On the contrary, difficult feelings you have been unconsciously holding may now come into awareness, exactly because the vigilant, controlling left-brain is inactive. This is to be regarded as beneficial, because these *suppressed* feelings are the major source of discontent, psychological dysfunction, and poor health. Uncovering and resolving them is the central concern in psychotherapy, and is what we are about in our use of art as a healing modality. The right-brain provides us with the power and perspective to work with these negative feelings. The left-brain, the thinking brain, can never resolve feelings; they must be engaged on the right-brain feeling level.

As we go deeper into the right-brain, we come to its most important quality, *witnessing*. Mystical consciousness and presence are founded in witnessing – the ability to detach and step back, to break the identification with the lower self, to transcend. The sense of witnessing is indispensable in working with feelings.

Left and right-brain directly relate to the metaphysical concept of a dualistic universe composed of apparently opposite but actually complementary qualities. In it, we are unable to know any one quality without knowledge of its complement: dark/light, up/down, space/solid, yin/yang, female/male. Dualism applies not only to the material universe but to our inner, feeling world as well. Thus, pleasure is balanced with pain; joy with sorrow; love with hate. There must be a place for both polarities – positive and negative – of any one dualistic pair for holistic well-being and spiritual maturity, although this does not condone the *acting out* of any negativity.

When we speak of the left-brained masculine mode, or the right-brained feminine mode, it's helpful to keep in mind that we are not referring to gender types, but to archetypal principles and energetic forces within us all. Both sexes possess male and female psychological qualities, and as we get to know ourselves better, we understand that to be true to ourselves, to be well-rounded, and to grow as a person, it is important to acknowledge, cultivate, and find a balance for opposite-sex psychological characteristics as well as same-sex qualities.

An important part of the path to consciousness is concerned with activating and balancing left and right-brain. This is accomplished by being aware of the different tendencies of the two sides of ourselves and making sure we utilize both, not necessarily at the same time, but aiming for an overall balance. Sometimes we may deliberately choose to cultivate a latent quality with which we are not yet completely competent, rather than just automatically apply a mode with which we are. For example, if we always make business decisions from the left-brain, we may want to begin introducing more of an intuitive approach to less consequential questions. If we always approach relationships as a nurturer, it may be important for us to move into a receiving or even more rational mode.

When balanced, both modes are active although one should dominate slightly. Severe problems occur when one mode tyrannically overpowers the other, either within an individual or in the collective as a reflection of individuals. In society today, we see such a grossly out-of-balance condition with the left-brain male archetype dominating and bringing the world ecologically and spiritually to the point of disaster. The notorious emphasis on progress, production, efficiency, the worship of rationality, reason, facts, science, technology, accompanied by the general minimization of feelings and the heart needs urgently to be brought into balance. However, it may be helpful to remember that it is not primarily men, but the masculine archetypal principle that has gotten out of control. Women may contribute to this collective imbalance by minimizing the female in themselves and worshipping the male principle, possibly unconsciously.

Both sexes, then, can be in need of developing the right-brain, feminine principle, which leads back to our main concern, art. That this has personal as well as global importance cannot be overemphasized.

## what is art?

Art begins in the realm of the right-brain, that place of feeling. Feelings include emotion, intuition, desire, pleasure and pain.

*Art occurs when feeling is portrayed in the material universe.*

As we participate either as viewer or creator in the art experience, we stimulate crucial right-brain creative capabilities that are often dormant and undeveloped in our society; we activate the right-brain to bring it into balance with the usually hyperactive, overemphasized left-brain. We start to become whole instead of only half a person. Not being whole within contributes significantly to the chronic unfulfillment and compulsive seeking outside ourselves that is common today.

But even though art originates in the right-brain, it would be a mistake to try to eliminate all influence of the left-brain. The left-brain assumes a critical part in the art process at the proper time, evaluating, editing, shaping. Artists with no left-brain skills run the risk of being ungrounded and unformed; the work can appear to have no direction or discipline. Learning how and when to combine both right and left-brain skills is crucial to the artist.

## John's story

In order to illustrate how we are set up to be frustrated by the left-brain indoctrination to which we are routinely exposed in our society, and how this can make an involvement in the arts all the more vital to our fundamental well-being, I'd like to share with you my story of how I was drawn to the arts. Although the details will differ from your own experience, it's quite possible there will be a commonality that may serve to awaken awareness in you of an unfulfilled passion, if that is what is needed.

My art story began in grammar school. Somewhere around eighth grade, I started becoming aware of myself. I noticed I'm bright and industrious, maybe even serious in contrast to most of my peers, who were basically into goofing off. I found it easy to achieve things. I won scholastic and activities awards. I started to establish an identity for myself related to these honors, and became achievement-oriented.

Everyone, relatives and friends of the family, was somewhat in awe of me and expected big things. My parents were of course proud. They wanted the best for me, an only child, and were dedicated to providing opportunities they never had as the children of working-class immigrants. They were advised that my high school education should be aimed at preparing me for a top-flight college. I was to attend a "country-day" prep school near our home in suburban New Jersey, about twenty miles west of New York City.

At first, in spite of my interest in doing well, I didn't want to go. I envisioned losing contact with my local buddies and being thrown in with a lot of uncool "brains." Moreover, even though I was an honors student, I had to attend summer school to make up for an alleged deficiency in reading comprehension. This hurt badly to my young growing ego and also because it meant not being able to spend the entire summer at our family's cottage at the then pristine Jersey shore.

Summers at the shore remain in my memory as idyllic – a childhood dream come true. Swimming in the ocean, boating on Barnegat Bay in my own boat, starting with a tiny one that I rowed incessantly from age ten, advancing to a small outboard-powered speedboat my parents bought for me in my teen years that opened the huge Bay for exploration and escape, I developed important qualities of self-reliance and confidence that carried over into adulthood.

But prep school became a good experience. I adjusted, I found friends, including some close ones. Academically, it was a well-rounded curriculum with emphasis on liberal arts as well as science. My performance here was average. I was no longer the big fish, I was surrounded by exceptional students. It was presumed we were the cream of the crop, that we would all be attending college.

I remember thinking as a child that I wanted to be either an architect or a psychiatrist, both potentially high right-brain activities. I had set up an old drafting table of my father's in the attic of our house, and in my private world would sit enraptured for hours designing houses, making sure to include smoke coming out of the chimney.

But when it was time to choose a college and career, I was advised to go into engineering. Engineering was the wave of the future and besides, I was told by my high school advisor with a wink, architects don't make any money. Since I always scored equally highly in both arts and science in the "aptitude" tests of the day, it made practical sense to choose engineering.

The psychiatrist aspiration had been killed even before high school when some well-meaning acquaintance of my parents told me that becoming a psychiatrist was not a good idea since I would have to become an M.D. first; rather, I should consider becoming a psychologist. As a child, I wasn't quite sure of the distinction. All I heard was disapproval, which tied into the lurking doubt, fear, and weak self-definition of my young mind, smothering the fragile buds of innocent soul aspiration.

So, after prep school, I entered Cornell University's School of Mechanical Engineering, proud of my accomplishment in having been accepted into one of the "top" engineering schools in the nation. Cornell was my personal first choice because of its wide spectrum of curriculum including liberal arts and architecture. I didn't want to be stuck in a school that was only technical, like many of the engineering schools. I wanted to have other intellectual influences around me.

And then, Cornell was coed. After having spent the last four years in an all-boys prep school, the idea of an all-male college engineering environment was highly depressing to my hyperactive, repressed, sublimated, teen-age sexual self. If there were not to be any girls in my classes, at least they would be nearby on campus. It was not for many years that I fully comprehended the impact of not associating with women as peers during those important formative periods. Women became objects of distance, fantasy, and unattainability well into my adult life.

Much of Cornell was stimulating – a new, wider world with unimagined resources and influences. I was right, it was important to be in a diverse environment. It was broadening to associate with students of the liberal arts, fine arts, architecture, even hotel management and agriculture, and I avidly took as many liberal arts classes as I could, in psychology, philosophy, and music. And there *were* women there, and I was able to be reasonably successful with them.

Of special importance to me was the fraternity experience. At that time, fraternities and sororities dominated campus social life.

My impression is that at present they are nothing like they used to be, and probably deserve whatever bad press they get. Then, however, it was different. My experience of the fraternity was one of genuine brotherhood. Founded on the ideal of brotherhood, taken seriously by us all, although we certainly knew how to party, it was a formative, deep bonding experience that started to address a need I was only vaguely in touch with, the need for spiritual community – a need which was to shape my direction in life but remain elusively unattainable.

However, in contrast to the enlightening social interaction was the actual experience of academia. It's still with bitterness that I recall it. Not knowing any better, trusting in the wisdom of the academic captains, driven by both the desire to achieve and the ever-present fear of failure, of busting out, I succumbed. I allowed myself to be run over by the tyranny. I do remember questioning it then, and getting answers such as "you are being trained to think." Yes, perhaps my mind was being sharpened, but it was pretty sharp to begin with – is this the only way one can be trained to think, and at what cost?

There were about two hundred of us in the School of Mechanical Engineering to start with. Right at the beginning, in our first orientation meeting on the first day, establishing fear as the prime motivator for "learning," the Dean of the M.E. School told us that only two-thirds of the present class would graduate from the five-year program, which turned out to be true. The way this information was presented was cute: "Look to your right, look to your left. One of you will not graduate."

With blind determination I vowed I would not be one of the failures. Getting kicked out of school was unthinkable. Everyone expected me to do well. My identity had been established as one who is superior – one who will be a success. I had been to prep school, conditioned into believing that to be without a college diploma foreshadowed a meaningless, wasted life as a factory worker or some other subnormal kind of existence. There was no option to graduating.

Driven by fear, I managed to be part of the group that graduated, but only because of a frenetic five-year effort in cramming. So ingrained became the fear that for much of my life I have had the recurring dream that I am back in college and have neglected to keep accurate track of my schedule as it changed each semester; overlooking and not attending a certain class, I will not graduate.

Then there was the curriculum itself – entirely theoretical and technical. A professor would walk into a lecture hall, start to write formulas on the blackboard, and stop only when the bell rang fifty minutes later, hardly speaking if at all. This was the typical "lecture." As students, our participation in the lecture was to copy what was written on the board, which of course was already printed in our textbooks.

The subject material covered such stimulating topics as calculus, differential equations, thermodynamics, materials analysis, fluids, heat transfer, dynamics, engineering physics, and so on. All was theory – deep technical theory no engineer would ever trust in building anything except possibly for NASA engineers calculating orbits.

I remember during one of my last years taking a class in internal combustion engines, with the expectation that at last I would learn something practical, something about cars. It turned out to be the same thing – a heavy dose of fuel/air ratios, compression analysis, rate of flame advance, Cárnot cycles, etc. I was even audacious enough to ask in class if we would ever be covering anything along the lines of how an engine actually works and was brusquely told by the professor to go to a trade school if I wanted to learn that sort of thing.

Was I in the wrong school – a school for rocket scientists? No, every engineering school in the country had basically the same curriculum and manner of teaching. It was customary to hear students talk about sticking it out just to get a degree and then going for an MBA to qualify for a really good job in the corporate world. Everyone so hated the experience that hardly anyone actually wanted to be an engineer; anyone who did was regarded as a geek, even then.

Totally absent was any concept of teaching by stimulating interest or creative involvement in problem-solving or invention; by showing the need for theory; in getting to know any student as an individual; in promoting any motive for participation other than fear. And not only was the material incredibly devoid of interest or relevance to what we might be doing as engineers if anyone were to try working at it after graduation – if they graduated – the work load was staggering. We studied literally every minute of the day and evening, all weekend, sometimes with "all-nighters," perhaps getting in some extra-curricular activity, taking a break one or two Saturday nights per month to completely blow out. And still, there was not enough time to really learn, understand, or appreciate anything.

Studying for exams in engineering school consisted largely of reviewing tests that had been given the last few semesters in the course and memorizing the correct response, which usually meant applying a formula to a theoretical case. Almost always, the exact same questions appeared. Files of previous tests were meticulously kept by fraternity members and passed down to younger brothers only; no one outside the fraternity had access to them. Of course, this was cheating, but I know I would not have graduated if I had not taken advantage of this resource, as everyone did. Amazingly, the professors never wised up, didn't care, or didn't have the energy to change the tests.

Recently I went to a college reunion, after not having been back for many years. I dropped by the engineering school, just to see if anything had changed. I expected to see a curriculum that would be unrecognizable but unbelievably, it was almost identical to what I had been presented with. Nothing had changed. I mentioned this to another returning alumnus, one who apparently did not share my extremist view of the Cornell academic experience. His reply: "I guess the basics will always be the basics."

During my time at Cornell there were momentous social changes afoot in the world. However, hardly anyone there had any awareness of this except for a few fine-artsies who staged an occasional happening, and the folk song club, which invited current folk artists to campus. There was no campus unrest, no protest, no demonstrations. But I was aware. I became aware of folk music and the philosophy that came with it sometime around my third year and immediately got hooked. My life was about to change. I bought a used acoustic guitar that I became deeply attached to and played every spare minute I could. Recoiling from depressive scholastic tyranny and deep soul sickness, my passion had been ignited.

At that time, in college, I could not have articulated what was going on in me. I didn't have the vocabulary to say that this intellec-tually repressive, fear-driven, achievement-oriented, hyper left-brain experience was starving and stifling an important part of me, an unrecognized and undeveloped part; that I was being worn-down; that being forced to resort to unscrupulous tactics had soured my idealism, making it clear to me I had no deep convictions; and that struggling for achievement all my young life, and the identity I had established for myself as a person bound for success, had removed me from my soul. I only knew I had a burning urge to play guitar and write songs.

Now, it's clear that inner guidance was trying to bring me into balance. There had been too much thinking, cramming, striving. The intellect had been dominant, and moreover had not been able to find satisfaction even on that level – there had been no real learning. The right-brain desperately needed to become active, and art is one of the languages, perhaps the main language, of the right brain.

I remain indebted to whatever part of myself it was that enabled me to respond to the inner voice – to buy the first guitar, to start playing, to follow my instincts, and eventually to make major life-style changes. Many hear the voice but do not respond, and sadly, many do not hear the voice at all.

# 2

# Taking In

*Exploring artistic perception;*
*Maximizing the viewing experience;*
*Establishing a spiritual practice*

This chapter is concerned with using art as a path to emotional healing and wholeness primarily as a *viewer*; the rest of the book will go into detail about the practice of *creating* art.

Art starts with *artistic perception*. The most important quality any artist can possess is artistic perception – to be able to open to an artistic stimulus and be moved by it. Then, art can touch parts of us – on an emotional, feeling level – that have been neglected or overlooked. We are transported to new universes beyond our conscious personal limits. We embark on fantastic excursions of imagery, drama, feeling, energy, and meaning.

Engaging art with this kind of heightened sensitivity is what makes art come alive, animated by the viewer. It's this same quality of being able to be moved by art, to animate it, that is essential to the artist creating, for this is how the artist works, and what accounts for the immense elation that accompanies the artistic act. The process of the artist is to experience and be moved by what has already emerged, and then to respond to that, building the piece.

It's essential to understand that it's our power that makes the art come alive. It's the responsibility of the viewer. The artist can create the most vibrant work of art, but if the viewer is asleep, there will be no art experience. The ability to open to art in this manner directly corresponds to the capacity for using art as an emotional/psychological healing path.

Exactly what is it that enables us to have powerful experiences with art, and why are some people more adept than others? There are several elements:

## concentration

The first basic attribute of artistic perception is *concentration*. Concentration is the ability to still the mind and focus exclusively on a single object. We think we see images before us, hear sounds in the air, read and comprehend thoughts printed in a book, but normally we perceive only a small percentage of what's available. Our incessant mental activity preoccupies us and blocks full perception not only of the outside material world but also the more subtle inner planes of consciousness and feeling. We are unable to silence the mind and observe from a place of clarity.

We should not be discouraged about this state of affairs. Rather, we must acknowledge that this is simply where we are on our evolutionary journey of consciousness. At our present stage our minds are relatively weak and lack capacity to focus – we use only a tiny percentage of the total latent potential of the brain. As we evolve, so advances our intelligence, emotional sensitivity, psychic capacity, and maturity in general. Artistic sensitivity represents a highly evolved consciousness, and consciously working to develop the psychic tools of the artist, such as right-brain awareness and the ability to concentrate, contributes immensely to our personal evolution.

When we acquire the ability to still and focus the mind, we can direct our attention like the beam of a searchlight, powerfully illuminating any object of interest; the doors of perception open easily; life takes on a new and wondrous tone; we become more sensitive and are moved by the most ordinary occurrences that previously passed by unnoticed; we gain the power to take in, *animate*, and become part of any art we so desire. Stilling and focusing the mind contributes greatly to the capacity for *presence* – the essential quality that makes art come alive as we view it, and imparts authenticity and power to its creation.

Stilling and focusing the mind is the first goal of any genuine spiritual practice. It is assumed we are unable to perceive Reality because of the wandering, chattering mind. Therefore, any spiritual practice that has the intention of training the mind will also, as a side benefit, bestow the ability to perceive art. You may have been involved in a type of meditation activity at some point. Perhaps you might renew your practice from a new perspective. And if you have been on a spiritual path without practicing any art, you may find that you have awakened artistic capabilities without so intending; it may be only a short step to picking up the paintbrush.

As thoughts quiet down, consciousness naturally shifts to another place, a place with a different sense of time. Being enmeshed in thoughts keeps us in a linear, time-bound mode; such is the nature of thought. Stilling thought brings us into the right-brain, into a timeless sense of being, where we vividly sense *the moment*, where presence becomes manifest. We begin to touch the edges of artistic consciousness.

## right brain

Stilling the mind automatically starts to shift you into the right-brain. You will start to experience yourself as more intuitive, feeling-oriented, non-judgmental, open. Intentionally try to approach art from this place. If you approach art with the left-brain orientation that is our most common mode – analytical, comparing, judging – you will get nowhere with art. You will be struggling to understand art instead of letting it act on you.

Art will act on you when you engage it with a non-judgmental, open mind. An open mind results when the mind is still and focused. Not only are restless thoughts absent, but pre-conceptions and prejudices are put aside so you can perceive the object as it is, instead of how you (unconsciously) think it is.

Observe your mind-state when you engage art. If you are still wrapped up in thoughts, try to put them aside. Consciously shift even more in the direction of right-brain feeling by becoming aware of yourself in your body. Becoming conscious of the body is one of the best ways I know to move into the right-brain. As you feel yourself in your body, become conscious of how body feeling might be extended to include any emotional feelings that may be present.

Continuing to relax, you enter the *alpha state* with the art. You are in a relaxed place, different from ordinary consciousness. You feel the art reaching out to you because of your openness. You start to feel yourself being moved by the presence you bring to the work. You feel nourished. As you bring presence to the work, you ready yourself to animate the work, to bring it alive, to experience it on a direct, energetic, feeling level.

## empathic viewing

Next, move into an empathic mode of perception. This is an extension of *concentration* and the right-brain orientation used by anyone who functions in humanistic capacities: artists, therapists, parents, lovers. To be empathic means to put aside your own thoughts and feelings and open to the stimulus before you, which in our case is a work of art, resonating with the feelings contained or reflected there. It is an intuitive skill that you will know how to activate once you form the intention.

The impulse to empathically engage objects outside ourselves naturally occurs at a certain point in our personal evolution. We understand the benefit of getting out of ourselves, of experiencing what the other is experiencing. We broaden ourselves as well as provide genuine energetic support when the object of our empathy is another person.

Empathic viewing of art is enhanced when we *identify* with characters or elements of the art – this is one of the keys to artistic perception. Think back to the Squat Theater performance. Put yourself in the place of any of the characters, feeling what they are feeling. For example, let's look more closely at the mannequin that has been hanging for an hour in the back corner of the stage. As you identify with it, you may first sense feelings of quietness, perhaps of dormancy, perhaps of being immune to or out of touch with life – it has been resting undisturbed by the chaos around it. Suddenly, its precious tranquility is ended by an unwarranted attack – people are throwing things at it just for amusement and as a vent for their hostility. Jarred out of its slumber, it is immediately put into a defensive posture, but it is really helpless – all it can do is thrash around in feeble protest, suspended on a hook, and then apparently give up, slumping into a lifeless coma. We feel fear, anger and outrage about being unjustly attacked, helplessness about our inability to defend ourselves, and ultimate despair and giving up. Note that it is not our feelings *about* the mannequin that we are cultivating, such as pity or protectiveness. We are attempting to get into the mannequin's space and actually experience what it is experiencing.

As you can see, there's a wealth of potential in just this small part of the production. Think what range of feelings are available in the segment where the young woman reads the erotic poem standing on the box. There's the sensual beauty of the visual scene and the actual spoken part – no less so because it is delivered in a language we do not understand. Empathically, we tune in to the erotic feelings being generated in her as she speaks. At the same time, she is courageously exposing herself. She is literally naked, throwing herself before us in a gesture of radical honesty – this is me – this is what I'm feeling. We are challenged to go beyond embarrassment, and to give our approbation. If we identify with her, we come in touch with the courage, vulnerability, and ultimate trust she embodies.

Not all feelings activated will be difficult, but difficult feelings are important because they represent suppressed negativity. Awakening these feelings is the first step in releasing them. As we empathically engage the breakfast scene, we may find feelings of peacefulness, motherliness, childhood. We may be touched by the tenderness portrayed. At the same time, we may be poignantly reminded of the absence of such qualities in our own childhood, or of other painful memories.

It's only because we have brought the powerful searchlight of our focused attention to these aspects that we experience so much. Many people will feel nothing, or if particularly repressed, will never be able to get beyond their indignation about the shocking nature of some of the scenes. Of course, our personal needs and tendencies will dictate which of these elements are important for us – which jump out because they stir up corresponding feelings in our subconscious.

One of my favorite lessons in the importance of empathic identification came from a description I read of a therapy session run by Fritz Perls, the founder of Gestalt Psychology. Fritz is working with a subject in front of a group. The subject dramatically relates a dream that takes place at the bottom of the ocean, with various characters acting on him, enticing and fighting with him. In the course of the description, he casually describes some objects lying there, including a rusty old automobile license plate. After hearing this complex dream, Fritz commands, "OK, be the license plate."

As you open with empathic identification, check once again to see if you are in the right-brain. Are you in a place where feeling, intuition, non-judgmentalism, acceptance, openness prevail? Remember you need not necessarily feel at peace to be in the right-brain. You could be empathically sensing any of the uncomfortable feelings just mentioned, but you will still be in the right-brain because of the way you perceive and remain present in the experience.

Empathically encountering art also provides a healthy vicarious experience that can contribute greatly to personal growth. We take in the experience of others and learn from it. We don't necessarily have to go through the same difficult learning circumstances ourselves. This has always been a central purpose of literature, but today may even more particularly apply to film, probably the most popular art form of our day. Film can be an incredible educational, growth-enhancing tool as long as we are careful to not use it as an escape, but as a means for broadening our experience, especially along emotional lines.

## open to feeling

As you empathically turn to the work, rather than seeking to get something from it or pursuing it, your stance is simply to be with it, to let it come to you, to move you. The relaxation of effort is key. As you stay with the work, contemplating it, illuminating it with the relaxed power of your concentrated attention, feelings are bound to come up.

Remain aware of the feelings as they are reflected in the art; honor them by giving them your full attention. Stay present with any feeling until it diminishes naturally or links to another feeling. Don't try to force the feeling to change or try to get rid of it. If the feelings are especially disturbing or painful, it signifies an important part of yourself has been touched, and it is all the more vital you stay with the feeling and not turn away from it in your discomfort. These are the feelings that have been buried in the subconscious and need to be brought into the light.

If the art has awakened a painful part of ourselves, we are likely to feel anger at the art, and to judge it as reprehensible or immoral, but it is essential to maintain a perspective. Blaming the art for the feelings it brings up is a knee-jerk reaction calculated to deny responsibility. We don't want to see that those feelings could be within us.

Some contemporary art may seem at first glance removed from feeling, and while this may be true in some cases, if we look closely, we usually will find that the art is still based on feeling. For example, abstract painting attempts to directly portray what is hidden behind the obvious exterior by showing energy and life processes. Swirling colors and distorted figures and patterns all have inherent feeling potential. Photorealism is the opposite of abstraction, and may appear at first to be only a display of skill, with no emotional content. But these images are usually carefully chosen, and may depict dark, decrepit, seamy aspects of society, for example. The implication here is that the dark feelings relating to these scenes must be accepted and integrated.

## do not interpret

Put aside any tendency to interpret, as well as evaluate, judge, compare, criticize, analyze, or even to understand the work. You may possibly question putting aside the tendency to interpret or understand, because we often believe that this is what is expected from us. Isn't the artist trying to tell us something, and aren't we supposed to get it? This kind of approach to art is the essence of the left-brain orientation. Immersed in the analytical left-brain, we leave the intuitive realm behind, and will never be acted on by art.

Meaning is not to be found through left-brain interpretation or intellectual understanding; meaning is to be found through *feeling*. Although it's possible, but by no means mandatory, that the artist in creating the art had a specific purpose in mind, if we try to analytically find that purpose, we do not experience the art. In order to experience the art we must open to it, we must let it work on us.

As we empathically open to the work on a right-brain feeling level, we have an experience of the piece. This experience will be a combination of what the piece may be said to objectively represent, if there is such a thing, and what we have projected onto it. We will not be able to discern between the two, nor should we try. Simply in surrendering to our experience, as it is, we enter the magical world of art.

## projection

The feelings that are roused when we empathically engage and identify with a work of art may correspond to what the artist intended to instill in the work. Usually, however, feelings will be highly skewed by what we bring to the art. We *project* onto the art, seeing in the work what is reflected from inside us, what is important to us. But this does not mean we are misinterpreting the work. On the contrary, it is our right as viewers to create our own meaning. Even if we have consciously stilled the mind in the effort to more clearly see the piece as it is and not overlay it with our own pre-conceptions, projection will still occur, only now, with a still mind, projection comes from a deep level.

Projection is an essential part of artistic perception. The experience of art must be highly subjective to be of value. Art serves as a stimulus to the subconscious, and brings forth what it might under the unconscious guidance of the higher self. If we surrender to this guidance, we trust that we are exactly where we should be in regard to the experience. We accept our experience, stay with our feelings, and let the art continue to work on us. In this way, we create our own valid meaning for the piece, but it is still a meaning based on feeling – it's what we *feel* that becomes the basis of the experience for us. At this point, we are *animating* the art – we are making it come alive.

*The exact moment when we project onto the art is when it becomes animated and alive; it becomes animated and alive precisely because we are projecting onto it.*

When a projection upon art is operative, feelings will come up spontaneously and abruptly. There may be a sense of the irrational about them – we are affected for no logical reason. The music we hear "makes" us sad, or the painting before us awakens a feeling of helplessness, and may not affect others the same way. What must be realized is that these feelings are coming forward from their trapped place in the subconscious, and the kinds of feelings we hold there may be different from other people's, but are eminently valid and must be honored.

These feelings in the subconscious form what is called the *shadow*, which can be understood to be the accumulation of unresolved negative feelings and impulses resulting from suppression on both a personal and collective level. On a personal level, each of us may have a bit more or less of any particular feeling, but on a collective level, we all share in the subconscious shadow that contains the complete realm of all possible human emotion.

A central purpose of psychological healing is to awaken, reveal, and release the shadow – this is why so many of the feelings we must engage are negative. As we let art work on us, these feelings, stored in the subconscious, will start to become apparent, through the projection mechanism. When a certain feeling is strongly or repeatedly awakened by any art stimulus, we know that this is a feeling that is coming forward to be cleared. If we allow ourselves to just be with the feeling, to watch it from a detached, impassive place as we experience it in the body without acting it out, it will clear.

## developing stillness

The following is a simple meditative technique for calming the chattering mind and replacing it with stillness, for developing concentration, and for moving into the right brain. Right now, try the following exercise for a period of thirty seconds:

Become aware of all thoughts racing through your mind.
Stop them.

You probably were able to perform the exercise to at least a certain extent, and you probably noticed a different kind of consciousness experience. For me, stopping thoughts usually sends me to the third eye, which is the psychic center for witnessing, among other things. I immediately become aware that I have been engulfed and lost in thoughts. I am jolted into greater awareness of myself. I remember myself. My sense of "I" is amplified. At the same time, the ability to focus my attention in whatever direction I choose is increased. If I send it towards an art object, the piece starts to come alive.

You may also have noticed how difficult it is to stop thoughts, once you take the time to become aware of them. It's quite normal that you will be able to stop thoughts for only a few seconds, and then become lost in them again, totally forgetting about what you are trying to do. This is one reason why we enter upon a dedicated practice – to cultivate this ability. Perform the exercise again, before peeking ahead to the next paragraph:

Become aware of all thoughts racing through your mind.
Stop them.

Notice what happened to your breath as you stopped thoughts. It's possible you also stopped breathing. This is obviously not what you want to do. Moreover, if you unconsciously associate stopping thoughts with stopping the breath, you will begin thoughts when you breathe. Try the exercise for a third time, with a modification:

Become aware of all thoughts racing through your mind.
Stop them.
Focus your awareness on the breath.

This puts you into a new place with stopping thoughts. You might begin to see how you could keep this up for a while. Now, you are practicing the basic Buddhist meditation: Sit with spine straight, still the thoughts, watch the breath and stay mindful – maintain the sense of non-engulfment, of witnessing, of waking up to yourself, becoming aware of yourself, of detached, passive observation. You are practicing stopping thoughts and focusing the mind together. Whenever you find yourself lost in thought, go back to watching the breath.

Having the breath as the object of your focus gives you an anchor, a place to put your attention, and also provides other psychic benefits. The quality of the breath (smoothness, deepness, capacity) is an indicator of consciousness in general. When you focus on the breath as it is, not trying to change it but just watching it with a sense of witnessing and acceptance, you start the psychic process of inner healing, clearing, and balancing, and the quality of your breath will change automatically over time.

Focusing on the breath as a meditative technique has another advantage over other methods in that it automatically brings you into the body. Since the body is the home of the feeling capacity, the right-brain is stimulated, and you will more quickly become aware of feelings hidden from awareness.

Your usual strategy in the meditation is to always return to focusing on the breath whenever you find yourself drifting off in thoughts, but there is an important exception to this, essential for both personal healing and the viewing of art. At some point, strong feelings may come up, usually connected with an inner image or memory of an incident, or even a fantasy. Now, instead of coming back to the breath you may choose to keep your focus on the feeling, using it as your meditative anchor, staying with the feeling, allowing it to deepen and reveal itself more fully. However, keeping an eye on the breath at the same time will stabilize you and help with the energetic resolution of the feeling. Try to keep 10% of your attention on the breath, and 90% on the feeling.

Strong feelings that come up in meditation as well as ordinary life or in relation to art represent attempts of the subconscious to clear itself, and should be recognized as such and given appropriate attention. If you allow the feelings to remain in awareness without judging them as good or bad, simply quietly watching and experiencing them, clearing will occur. In contrast, the wandering thoughts of the mind are just the result of the mind's lack of development and do not represent suppressed material coming into awareness.

# 3

# Starting

*Getting organized on the art path;*
*The personal in art; The need for original expression;*
*Combining art and the spiritual path*

When I left college I was seriously primed for a major re-alignment experience. But I was not ready to walk away from engineering just yet. Work would be different from school, I reasoned, and I was anxious to get out in the world and put my degree to use. Surprisingly, I found I enjoyed the first job I got, through on-campus recruiting, in the plant engineering department of a major corporation in Philadelphia. I had to design equipment and systems, supervise fabrication and installation of them, and got to see right there whether it worked or not. It was creative, in the inventive sense, and sort of fun, and I was good at it. I liked my boss and worked well with him.

But I was right, there was nothing, absolutely nothing I learned in college that prepared me to do this job, unless you insist I was "trained to think." The most useful education from all my schooling was a mechanical drawing class I had in prep school. Rather, I believe it was just a strong mechanical aptitude that mercifully had not been killed by college tyranny that I was applying.

Yet, I was unsatisfied. I could envision spending my whole life in the corporate environment, mildly fulfilled in my work, but leaving this other side of myself that had been stirred never fully realized. Is this what I wanted? Just as I had to at least try engineering, I knew I had to try to follow this other dream – this dream of music, of being an artist. Other people were doing it, why not me? What if my whole life went by and I never heeded such a compelling impulse? And I knew I could never get where I wanted just doing it part-time, on the weekends – I needed to dedicate myself to it.

After a year on the job, I emotionally told my boss I was quitting. I remember he told me what I needed was a wife and a mortgage. Maybe he was right

The decision to leave Philadelphia was made much easier by a visit to New York to check out the art scene. After fifteen minutes of walking around on the streets, seeing the women who were there, my mind was made up – this was where I had to be, this wasn't Kansas anymore. However, I was still not ready to make the complete leap. I got another engineering job in New York, in technical sales, which had a glamour attached to it that attracted me, along with the potential for high money. But this job didn't go well. I could never apply myself to learning the huge amount of technical material needed, my boss was a scoundrel (an enlightening experience in itself), and I never sold anything. I quit after six months, and have never had regular employment since.

Making such a radical shift in life-style was not something done easily or lightly. It meant taking a sharp turn from the path I had been on; finally admitting that the preparation I had was irrelevant to what I thought I wanted to do, but not knowing how long I would continue to want to do it; leaving behind the security of a regular paycheck. None of my friends from college or prep school, except for one, made any similar changes. They all continued to move forward into the establishments of the corporate-business-academic world.

I found it hard to want to remain in contact with most of my previous friends, feeling that I could never explain what I was doing, that they would think I was a failure, and that we had nothing in common any longer. I found their aspirations of material success distasteful; their consciousness unenlightened.

As an artist at large in New York, I needed to make a living, but it had to be something that left time for my art. After trying a few different self-employed activities, I settled into being a woodworker. I started by building shelves in apartments, advertising myself with flyers posted on the street. Eventually, I became more professional, getting my own shop together, designing and building custom furniture and cabinets. This fit in perfectly with the ethic of manual labor that was part of the counter-culture: working with the body in order to get back into it and out of the head. That I was also working as a designer satisfied my architectural side. I was consciously applying both left and right-brain, and it felt good.

Although I never made much money as a craftsman, money was not the object. By keeping expenses low, I was able to divide my time equally between woodworking and music. I'd focus on a construction project for a week, and then spend the next week full-time on music, or until the next project rolled in. I found it even helped to have another unrelated activity to turn to, to get away from the music. I found this life-style fulfilling, and continued it for ten years.

My understanding of the implications of physical labor kept growing. I saw how working with the body deepens the connection to the feeling nature, centered in the body. I also liked working by myself. I was able to experiment with using the work as a vehicle for meditation, which was an invaluable self-training. Staying conscious of the body as it performed tasks, watching as a *witness*, would powerfully bring me into the moment. I felt myself becoming grounded, balanced, at home and fascinated by the evolving counter-culture around me with its emphasis on consciousness and self-inquiry in which I participated fully.

But it was music that was my passion. Feeling I was a late-bloomer, I pushed myself even harder than a Capricorn might usually. All my efforts were focused on writing songs, practicing, performing in public - cautiously at first, but then getting regular jobs in bars as a singer/guitar player. I took the ambition I might have put into corporate or material achievement and re-directed it into artistic channels.

However, there were two sides to the ambition. I wasn't quite aware how much I was driven for personal success, probably more so than many of the previous friends to whom I could no longer relate, and whose lives I disdained as mundane, establishment-oriented, and in the extreme, money-chasing. I wasn't quite aware that part of me was using my new identity as an artist to bolster my ego – to set me apart, to show that I was better, more sensitive, feeling, that I was more evolved, maybe even to compensate for a fear of not being able to compete in the corporate world. This part of myself would strive relentlessly at my art until I was recognized.

But I don't regret any of it. This is how we begin. The ego-drive must be honored and given freedom to express itself, especially when we are young. To repress this basic impulse leads to soul-sickness. To be an artist doesn't necessarily mean to be without ego – often, just the opposite is true – it just means that it's natural to want to become a success, to be recognized, to achieve as an artist, and not as something else. At this point, at an older age and after much time spent exploring the "spiritual," I must confess that the impulse for success and recognition is still with me, although hopefully I am no longer primarily motivated by it and have found a place where I can co-exist peacefully with it.

## the fringes

After we have had enough experiences with art as a viewer, we may be tempted to try our hand at creating. The time it takes for us to pick up the paint brush, sit down at the piano, get the lap-top in shape, sign up for acting class, get our hands in the clay, or start sewing toe-shoes will vary between individuals. Some may start with no hesitancy at an early age and show a precocious talent.

Some may spend a life-time as a highly sensitive viewer, but never make the jump to that of a doer.

It's interesting that prior to activating strong interests and talents many people find themselves in oppressive, opposing circumstances – not only in the arts, but in all areas of life. It seems to be more than just coincidence, as if some kind of karma is creating the opposition from which they will rebound with extra-normal ability and passion, if they can meet the challenge.

Often, we find ourselves on the fringes of the art world, attracted and connected in some way but without the confidence to participate as an artist. We may even become business professionals in the arts – agents, managers, lawyers – but still we do not create. Often, however, this is how we move into the arts and how we develop sensitivity. This was the case with me.

In college, when I first was strongly attracted to the guitar and singing, I had absolutely no confidence. I knew I was passionate about music, but the idea of playing for anyone was highly traumatic. I was a closet artist. I remember when I wrote my first song. Of course it was dismally unsophisticated, but I was not aware of this. I was swept up by the euphoria of the creative act, flying high. I took my guitar over to my girlfriend's place. She was quite the arty type, a jazz singer in off-campus night spots and a painter – a good example of how we can be attracted to others who are active in the arts, who carry the projection of that unborn part of ourselves that needs to be stirred.

I was so high with creating the song that I found the momentary confidence to sing it to her, sitting on the lawn outside her parent's house on a fine spring afternoon where she lived. After hearing it she said, "Do you realize that song has only two notes?" This was not the reaction I was planning on. I crumpled. It was to be many years before I would share original music again. Of course, she could have been more generous. I didn't realize at the time that she represented a type of woman with whom I was to continually become involved – beautiful, magnetic, talented, but without heart. I mistook charm for love, a reflection of my own lack of heart. On a deeper level, I can see now that her absence of support was only a reflection of the self-doubt I carried within; that's why I bought into her statement and let it affect me so profoundly instead of laughing it off, and perhaps why I attracted such a person to begin with.

Other kinds of roundabout involvements with the arts were to occur before I found the confidence to step out on my own. My roommate and good friend in my fourth year at college was an excellent musician and leader of a twelve-man acappella singing group. Without confidence and no real ability yet as a singer, but being attracted to the group I became their business manager, setting up dates and handling money, all the time feeling left-out as I would travel with them and watch them perform.

Then, shortly after college, soon after I arrived in New York, I repeated the experience by falling for and moving in with a young ballerina – my second great love – who had been dancing from the age of five and was now performing professionally with New York City Ballet at the ripe-old age of seventeen. I spent the next few years constantly watching ballet from the guest box, fascinated not only by the art but with the world of dance itself, including all the juicy insider details about the twisted lives of the dancers in the company and company politics under the direction of the contro-versial George Balanchine. Especially enlightening was the intro-duction to the homosexuality in the dance and art world for me, a straight boy with an Ivy League, ivory tower background.

All during this time I was learning, but I was smothered; my music was strictly in the closet. There was no way I could perform in front of these talented professionals. It wasn't until about five years after college, after this relationship had ended, that I began to come out and start performing in public.

Our confidence is usually based on our appraisal of our talent. We often doubt if we have enough of it. Others seem talented – they are the ones who should be doing, but not us. But what is talent?

## talent

Capacity develops in any field through interested involvement and practice. By practice, I don't mean practicing scales. I mean getting to the point where art has meaning for you now, doing art based on an emotional involvement, not learning by rote. If there is any validity to the theory of re-birth, as I believe there is, talents are carried over from life to life. Someone who is born with "talent" is just someone who has been developing that capacity in previous life-times. The eminent Indian musician Ravi Shankar has said that the talent to become a master musician can be developed in six lifetimes. Only six lifetimes? If this is true, and if I really want to be an artist, what's stopping me?

So how do we begin? As a child, I was given piano lessons, where I would sit and diligently try to read notes on paper, and then later in the high school band I played saxophone, reading my part. But none of this woke my passion. It was the same approach to learning I was to endure in college, dryly focusing on the technical with no concern for emotional involvement. It left me uninspired and unmotivated.

Passion for me did not come until I made a true connection to music, to something that moved me, which started with Elvis and fully blossomed with folk and rock music. That's when I put the sheet music away and started playing from the heart. Then, if I needed to learn something that was written or if I needed to develop a technical skill to express what I was feeling, the motivation was there to read and drill. Discipline became self-discipline, founded on passion.

Usually, the passion is awakened by someone else's art. We are so moved that we simply must take part. We learn the songs that move us and we sing them; we learn the painting style of a certain master and emulate that; we have writers who are our gods and their voice speaks through us. This is how we begin making art.

Following our passion, we awaken our artistic right-brain capacity, bringing it into balance with our left-brain thinking, reasoning side. We take important steps to regaining the wholeness that our left-brain culture has all but stamped out. We feed that part of ourselves that has been starving. We open the door that allows a higher force to enter and shape the art under our fascinated attention. Our feelings and intuition are stirred, our sensitivity enhanced just by participating in the art, and it feels good. And it does not matter what our level of "talent" is; it is by forgetting about how much talent we have and allowing ourselves to be fully swept away by the experience that talent develops.

## the personal

We live in a most unique period of history. Our world is changing at an unprecedented rate. We are presented as perhaps never before with continual challenges to our deepest identity and stability that result from these changes; but we are also presented with remarkable opportunities for individual growth.

Nowhere has this dichotomy manifested more strikingly than in the fields of art and technology. Both art and technology have undergone incredible progress and evolution in the last several hundred years, differentiating them from the previous thousands of years of known history. In fact, I would suggest that we view the progress in art as an exact parallel to the progress in technology. It's also easier to understand the full significance of the art revolution if we keep the technological in mind.

What has happened in art, what the incredible revolution has brought, is that art has become *personal*. As technology has brought the impersonal – the assembly line with its mass production of identical products and corporate environment – art has tried to serve as the balance, moving us more into the individualistic, helping us re-establish the personal identity that has become threatened by these powerful social influences. Even though many people may not seek out art directly, the art revolution has significantly affected us all through its influence on mass media, TV, music, and film, where we see the same growing focus on individual, personal experience.

The period of the Impressionists, coinciding with the dawn of the Industrial Age, roughly marks the beginning of the personal in art. Of course, the personality of the artist has always permeated art, but it was usually not considered to be the point of the work, only a distinctive signature. With Impressionistic painting, the revolution began. The focus of the work started to shift from the subject portrayed to the artist, and particularly to the feelings of the artist. Typically illustrating commonplace scenes – landscapes and the like – the artist's feelings soared through in the use of color, texture, brushwork, style. And not only were feelings of brightness captured in the work but, most importantly and perhaps for the first time, the darkness of the human soul was portrayed. These artists themselves may not have been completely aware of the immense historical significance of the shift in their approach to artistic expression.

Before this period, art had been largely impersonal and a reflection of the values of the group. In early times, people existed primarily as members of a larger body, and the actual experience of individual consciousness may have been quite different from that of today. The most common, and often only application of art in any given early culture was in a religious or mystical context, and here it was largely intended to inspire. Aside from this, art may have served to depict what was considered to be the beautiful, the heroic, the ideal, or a similar abstract theme, a direct result of its use in religion. Art also served, in its less esthetic application, as illustration or record-keeping. No matter what century we look to, we generally see art used in these impersonal ways, especially Western art.

As we survey Eastern art of the past, which is of interest because we are much influenced today by Eastern thought in our approach to healing and consciousness work, we see a parallel. The Eastern conception of religious or mystical realms is different from the Western, but still there appears to be an absence of the personal in the art and an emphasis on representation of deity. We may also see the representation of emptiness, or transcendence, or inner equanimity in the art of the East, but still, it is an abstract ideal that is portrayed.

What a contrast from contemporary art! Today art has branched off into myriad categories and genres. We have art for social awareness, for satire, for teaching, for self-revelation, for portrayal of psychological types, for portrayal of the archetypes of human consciousness both positive and negative, to celebrate, to stimulate, to provoke, to mourn, to display cleverness, inventiveness and skill, to evoke moods, to suggest other modes of being and view-points and so on, but most importantly, we see that art is largely intended to communicate personal experience. And among the most powerful kind is that which communicates feelings – the personal feelings of the person making the "art." Think about it: This kind of art, this use of art to communicate inner feelings, sometimes very intimate feelings, has been with us only for a short few hundred years.

And why would someone want to display their feelings in public, and why would someone else be interested in seeing these feelings displayed? Because art today is the reaction, the dualistic complement, to the technology in which we are immersed. As technology has dehumanized us, made us identical consumers and put us into little boxes, there has been a rebellion through that aspect of the collective consciousness that we call "the artist." The function of the artist in society today has become to rescue the soul, to bring it to light – particularly the dark and ignored side of the soul – and today that soul is suffering in historically unique ways. The emergence of individuality is being directly stimulated by the oppressive technical culture; the soul needs to break out of the stifling isolationism in which it is trapped; art has become one way it seeks to do this.

So when a poet howls in pain, it is interesting to us because it tells us that the unconscious and conscious pain we feel is not unique to ourselves; others feel the same thing. It tells us that our pain is real, and justified, and suggests that something can be done about it. We find that the act of sharing art contributes greatly to the resolution of the pain and isolation. Often, we hide our pain for many different reasons: shame, pride, insensitivity, ambition, busyness, ignorance. As we see the most personal aspects of another's pain as well as joy, it puts us in touch with those similar aspects in ourselves that we may have overlooked; our awareness is greatly facilitated. And as we recognize that pain is common, we are encouraged to take the next step to psychological healing, acceptance. If we consciously apply ourselves to creating art that works on this level, we can use art as a most powerful vehicle for our personal consciousness work.

However, sometimes art today can indeed seem impersonal, and over the last twenty years we have seen something of a backlash against the personal in art. Much of the painting that is hung in galleries today appears to emphasize technological process and to avoid personal information. But the personal element in art is overall still strong in today's culture. In dramatic film, the most popular art form of the day, the trend toward emotional realness continues. In documentary film and TV, today's "reality" shows, aside from their artistic merit or tastefulness, have reached new levels of personal feeling disclosure and audience involvement. In rap, the most popular music of the day, the candid personal element in the lyrics, the rage and pain, have been responsible for its success, even through the emotional expression here, I would venture, is blameful and unenlightened. If you are an artist working in any media, you will be able to include the personal in your art, once you understand the importance of it and desire to do so, and it will stand a fair chance to be appreciated.

Looking at our current period of history, we also see the unique emphasis on consciousness and healing. Information is routinely available on the shelves of bookstores that was, since the beginning of civilization, kept guarded in secrecy in order to avoid persecution for its possession. Now, this information is almost common knowledge except that, of course, the higher comprehension is still available only to those who are developed enough to see. Nonetheless, we live in a period of tremendous, unprecedented opportunity. The time is favorable for deep, productive, inner work, and we can make huge leaps in our evolution, combining healing with art. I personally view the imposing crisis-climate in which we live as the emergence from the group soul of long-repressed negativity. If we take advantage of the time, and if we know how, we can release the negativity as it comes into awareness.

What all this amounts to is that I want to encourage you to take your art to a personal level – only in this way can art become deeply healing. This highly unique historical period of heightened consciousness work and the inclusion of personal feelings in what we call "art" can be greatly used for your benefit.

## original expression

To take the practice of making art to a personal level means your art must contain original expression. It's true we see many great performers executing the compositions of others with exceptional sensitivity and skill, particularly in the music and theater worlds. Parallel with this orientation in the visual arts may be artists who portray representational, outer images rather than original, inner images. It may be presumed that these artists identify with these roles and images, and with the feelings that they invoke. They make the roles and images their own, they find themselves in them, they interpret them in a stylized manner, moving into deeper personal awareness through them.

But it's a fact that many musicians, especially classical musicians, are unable to play two notes without a piece of paper in front of them; many painters are unable to paint without an outside form to portray. They may have developed great technical skill but are unable to connect the skill with anything inside – they have nothing to say, and so fail to invite deep interest. Contrast this with a jazz musician or abstract painter whose mode is primarily improvisation – of letting art spontaneously emerge as it is performed. Who would you say is moving closer to the subconscious and discovering parts of themselves through their art?

I would hold that until you begin to directly express your own feelings, visions, ideas and suppressed self in your art, the art will not be used for personal healing and growth. And when you do, the issue of technical skill becomes irrelevant. Art is not about having skills; it's about allowing the subconscious to emerge. Some of the best art can be done by artists with low skills, and there have been art movements that have been anti-technique, deliberately minimizing technical skill in favor of allowing feeling to come forward through the media.

An unexpected example of the importance of using art for personal growth can be found in the career of Bob Dylan, which also illustrates typical developmental stages of artists. In a brilliant biography by Anthony Scaduto (Grosset and Dunlap 1971), we get a in-depth picture of Dylan's life and motivation. With a career that peaked during an eight year period starting in 1962, he played a critical role in shaping not only the course of popular music, but in significantly influencing social conscience through his protest songs.

Dylan's fascination for pop music was awakened in high school by an intense attraction for and identification with the earliest of the rock and roll icons: Bill Haley, Elvis, Buddy Holly, but especially Little Richard. Dylan started playing self-taught piano, singing in the style of Little Richard – wild, raucous, screaming. He became good enough in this style to perform locally with a group behind him. His stated goal was to become an entertainer – to be as big as Presley. There is yet no sense of artistic self-definition, as he models himself after an idol.

After a few years, society and music have changed, and Dylan finds a new model, Woody Guthrie, the legendary itinerant folk-singer from the 'thirties. He falls for Guthrie so completely that he takes on a Guthrie persona – backwoods, inarticulate, rootless, wandering across the face of America, simple and heartfelt. He arrives in New York with this persona polished and intact, interpreting Guthrie-type songs of the past in his performance. Guthrie was one of the first protest singers, but his protest was closely tied to the labor movement, the issue of his times. Dylan at first adopted these themes in his music, leaning basically into the past, still with the goal of "making it" with this musical style as his vehicle.

As the biography describes, it was almost accidental that Dylan latched onto the protest theme as an expression of rebellion against what was happening currently, Vietnam. When a girl friend of his tells him of some other singers who are experimenting with this form, it appears to him that it might be another good avenue to try in his bid for stardom. We see that he is ego-driven, but there is nothing wrong with this; it provides the motivation to produce. When he turns to writing the protest song of his day, he leaves behind the Guthrie roots; he jumps to a new level of artistic integration; he becomes current; and somehow, genius has occurred. The songs he produces over the next few years will help to turn a nation around. His ego drive has been used by higher forces, and art has happened. For anyone who has been moved by his songs, it makes no difference whatever that he created a stage persona. These are the tools of the ego that prepare for inspiration. The songs themselves are brilliant beyond words – in composition, social significance, and artistic value.

I remember attending a Dylan concert during my last year in college, when he was just starting out. The theater, an old movie house, was about 20% filled on a dull, drab Sunday afternoon in Syracuse, New York. At the time, I completely bought into the stage character that set him up to deliver those unforgettable songs. The performance was unprecedented for me. It was an artistic experience of opening the heart. I remember a woman behind me sobbing during the songs. It was the very first time I had ever seen anyone moved to tears at a performance. I was astounded and moved as well.

From the biography, we learn what was behind Dylan's ground-breaking shift to folk-rock, which essentially signaled the end of the folk era. Dylan became disillusioned by the protest movement, believing in the end that it was not possible to deeply change people's hearts by singing songs to them. And moreover, that the movement itself only strengthened and perpetuated the very forces it was aligned against. Upon first hearing this viewpoint, it may sound like a cop-out, a justification for lack of courage to continue the fight, a giving-up. That's probably the way I would have thought of it back then. But now, I see it differently, and I find myself understanding and agreeing with his viewpoint.

What Dylan became aware of was that the protest movement was self-defeating because it was based on condemnation and blame, even though that blame seemed eminently justified because it was aimed at apparent evil. When we blame, we overlook the deeper reality that we all share responsibility for what is happening. The violence that was being acted out was a result of hatred having built up in the collective subconscious shadow. Blaming prevented that realization. We didn't face the real problem, which was the evil in our own hearts.

Dylan became aware that he had indeed sacrificed himself in his art. His art was only a product – a very beautiful product – in which he was trying to achieve goals. The foremost goal was the creation of the protest message in service to society, and the deeper ego-goal was to achieve personal stardom. He felt like he had wasted his energies in serving these false goals, and was bitter. He felt like he needed to turn his energies towards serving his real needs, starting with nurturing himself, and then using art as a means to uncover and understand himself – as a tool for self-discovery and healing – in his condition of psychic sickness that had resulted from the severe pressures of stardom and his fierce ambivalence towards it. In making this shift, and in leaving product-oriented art behind, he felt like he was being true to himself in going back to his original musical roots, rock music, which he incorporated into the "folk-rock" sound.

Dylan turned to inner-directed, self-exploratory art. Even though his art had been original all along, it still did not focus within, on his own feelings. The second half of his body of work during that eight-year period represents this shift. Many of his followers did not get it; he was often booed off stage when first presenting the new format, but he kept with it because he realized he had no choice. He had seen the limitations of outer-directed artistic work, and needed to bring it to a more personally significant level. He needed to find his soul.

In what ways do you avoid using your art as a pathway to the soul? Do you use it for commercial purposes, thinking that you are an artist and never realizing what is lacking? Do you have an ulterior purpose for the art that keeps it from really touching you, that keeps you editing out everything except that which you think will be acceptable to your audience? Are you pre-occupied with technical ability, and making an impression? Are you ready to drop any such outward orientation and use your art primarily for your own benefit – to heal and know yourself – as a vital tool to self-discovery?

## art, the spiritual path, and psychology

What is the spiritual path?

Sometimes, we are moved to search for something larger than ourselves to hold us up. Those who have found such support within the context of traditional religious formats tell us we all need to make this connection; by ourselves, as isolated souls struggling against the world, we can never know happiness. The essence of this approach is to find the omnipotent source outside ourselves – God – and to place ourselves in psychic relation to it so we receive its blessings. Sometimes we hear artists who have been awakened by the intense inner focus of art say they have become more spiritual, they have found a connection to God.

But for various reasons, maybe primarily my personal psychological make-up, I have never been entirely comfortable with the traditional concept of God, even though I think of myself as a spiritual person. My spiritual leanings are in the direction of the Eastern "religions," although these are not usually religions in the sense that one might think, coming from a Western Judeo-Christian background with its central concept of God.

In Buddhism, which a vast percentage of the world's population follows, there is no mention of God, nor of needing to find something outside oneself. Instead, it is essentially taught that left-brain preoccupation must be dropped in order to reach higher consciousness and enlightened psychological functioning, which takes place as one moves into *the moment* of the right-brain.

It's further understood that the hyperactivity of the left-brain, especially the aspect of continual *striving*, is instrumental in creating and perpetuating the sense of the limited ego and its associated pain, which is a fundamental problem addressed in Eastern psychology. The ego is considered to give rise to the experience of isolation and existential discontent that is to be outgrown by means of spiritual practice. Going beyond the experience of the limited ego-self is the goal of all Eastern spiritual disciplines, and begins by shifting into the right-brain, with the aid of meditative practices such as we discussed in chapter two.

The emphasis of Eastern spiritual paths is to give us an experience – a transcendental experience – that will result in our becoming enlightened beings. We see a "higher" reality for ourselves, and our actions become automatically modified according to our perception. There is no need for belief, or for dogma, or for any authority to tell us how to live our lives.

Moreover, in contrast with finding and connecting to a being larger than ourselves, outside ourselves, the path is one of going within, of *self-realization*, to discover more and more of ourselves. As we keep expanding our awareness of who we are, we come to a point of recognizing that we are beings with a vaster, more cosmic potential than we are now aware of, that we are essentially all one, and that we will come into contact with a higher power, a renewing source within us – not outside of us – that will sustain us. The journey of expanding inward is the evolutionary path we are all on, whether we know it or not.

It is this philosophy of expanding inward, of self-realization, that aligns the spiritual quest with the psychological and art quest so they all become one path. We do not need to distinguish between spiritual values and beliefs, our psychological life, and the art we make. The emphasis of psychotherapy has always been concerned with going inward, bringing light to the shadow, releasing suppressed feelings. Consciously applying these principles to your art, you practice a form of self-therapy. As you use your art to go within, to discover and integrate parts of yourself that have been suppressed from conscious awareness, you are proceeding on the spiritual path, and the art process itself becomes meditation. Consciously combining all three paths results in a discipline that provides a most powerful vehicle for personal evolution, while each path by itself will be less effective:

Spiritual paths of the East are not usually concerned with personal feelings and are not prepared to deal with them even though they teach how to still the mind and prepare for the emergence of super-consciousness. Psychotherapy, while interested in feelings, does not usually include the altered states that meditation brings about, in which feelings are easily accessed, and does not usually teach the true acceptance of them that is part of the spiritual path. The artist may be working with feelings, but may not understand the psychological and spiritual subtleties necessary to successfully engage them.

The common ground on which all three paths – art, spirituality, and psychology – meet is the emphasis on *feelings*, and most especially the dark, difficult feelings that linger in the subconscious. This is where we start. When first attracted to the idea of expanding consciousness to include transcendent realms, we are apt to make a common mistake. We tend to look for something grand, minimizing or ignoring the dark aspects inside ourselves. We may not be clear about what this something grand is, except that we expect it may manifest as a sense of peace, contentment, or love. But avoiding the important dark aspects of the self, justified by a quest for the light, leads only to more suppression and hypocrisy. Including these feelings in our art, as part of our personal process, leads both to the inner psychological healing and spiritual realization that we seek.

This practice is meant to be undertaken as a lifetime path – it changes and develops us slowly. We grow as a flower does. Power and clarity of mind, the refinement of personality, the maturing into an evolved being, the sense of presence, the ability to manifest through the art, emotional clearing, all take place slowly. We cannot rush the process, but if we are maintaining a steady practice, it becomes apparent when change has taken place. We are different now from five years ago, or even one or two years ago. We are different from what we would have been if we had not been practicing. And if we are new to the work, it is true that we may experience radical jumps in consciousness quickly, even after only a month or two.

Remember, the path must be traveled with a sense of dropping striving of any sort, even striving for the spiritual experience, enlightenment, for love, or for God. Rather than striving, cultivate the sense of *acceptance*, primarily in regard to your feelings, as they are. Striving is what the ego is good at. Merely shifting the object of striving to some imagined and projected "spiritual" goal does not change us. We remain self-oriented, deficient, and coming from lack.

The key is to learn how to be supported and nurtured by your practice *now*. Then, you will not approach it as a duty, or a means to get anything or anywhere. You will be content in the present, conscious of presence, and your growth will take place steadily and surely.

# 4

# Opening
# The Door

*Accessing the artistic subconscious; Moving inward;*
*Understanding how healing occurs; Finding your voice;*
*The NOW practice*

In order to bring art to the level where it has personal significance, where it is a reflection of our own depths and can become instrumental in our quest for wholeness and healing, we must learn how to connect it with the subconscious. Not all art is healing; not all creativity is art. It will be helpful to understand these three distinct processes before we put them all together into one.

## the creative process

The creative process is not necessarily the same as the art process. Creativity may or may not lead to art, but art always contains creativity. As I sit writing this chapter, I am being creative. I assemble all sorts of thoughts from many different sources into a hopefully cohesive, linear expression. At best, I may be talented and even artful in my expression, but I would not call this type of writing art.

*Art happens when subconscious feeling enters the creation.*

I began to work on this chapter by sitting for a while, perhaps a half-hour, staring at my blank computer screen with a vague idea of what the chapter would be about. I did not strive or push myself to come up with anything. Soon, however, thoughts came into mind; I had the key sub-headings in place. As I started to write under each of the sub-headings, more thoughts came. Sentences formed. Miraculously, most of them were coherent. After a certain amount of writing, the need for some reorganization became apparent. When I put aside the work for the day, went to sleep and woke the following morning, new thoughts were there about where the work should go next, about important points that should be included that I had not thought of before.

Who is creating the work?

Even though I get to put my name on the front of the book, anyone skilled in the creative process knows that it is both "I" and "not-I" who has created the work. "I" refers to the conscious ego-I, the one with the plans. "Not-I" refers to that other self of whom I am only partially aware. That's the self who does the creative stuff. What "I" do is basically housekeeping. "I" feed the body, provide a space, arrange for quiet time, fix the computer. "I" figure out what we are aiming for and ask the questions – in themselves important steps. In addition, "I" can provide the basic motivation for the work, as we have seen with regard to Dylan. But then I turn it over to "not-I" who presents the ideas and answers, something "I" has not thought of and won't. Then, after the ideas have been presented, "I" will again get involved as an editor, doing the grunt work that "not-I" is too finicky and delicate to perform.

There is some other part of me that does the creative work. I have learned that it's my job to set up conditions and then get out of the way, to wait. Getting out of the way means quieting the mind as we have touched upon – coming into the moment, putting aside thoughts of the future or past, being here now, making a space for the unfoldment to occur. This approach is identical to the spiritual quest, where we are taught that we must prepare the soil for grace to descend, but that we cannot really do anything to invoke grace. On the contrary, all thoughts of striving and trying of the conscious ego-mind will only impede the flow of grace. It is through surrender that grace comes. Grace is being touched by something beyond our conscious self. It brings clarity and peace and creativity.

Some people have experienced what is referred to as "channeling," where creativity is transmitted from some other specific personality of another dimension. There is no doubt channeling is possible. Just looking at the wisdom in the material that has come through in well-known cases, such as *A Course in Miracles*, or the work of Alice Bailey, the medium who wrote at the turn of the century, is enough to convince that another intelligence is at work. In channeling, the one receiving the work is usually aware of the personality transmitting it. Most authentic cases of channeling, by the way, occur with women because their natural receptivity makes them the best mediums, which is what channeling is; surrendering to and allowing another intelligence to come through.

Some may associate the ultimate source of our creativity with God. As I have stated, I view the spiritual path as a journey into myself, a path of self-discovery, and that these gifts of the spirit that come from beyond my conscious mind are only from some other part of myself yet to be fully recognized. I have never consciously channeled any writing or art from a discarnate personality, although the possibility remains that such a source has been helping me without my awareness. My experience has always been that, yes, there is a creative power outside myself on which I rely, but it is my larger, my higher self. This is the essential message of Eastern philosophy.

Pragmatically, an important ability to enhance creativity is to be able to recall your dreams in detail. If you take care to try to remember your dreams upon awakening, writing them down, for example, you will build the capacity for recall and for getting inspired information. In studies of all types of creative people, most have said they get many if not most of their inspired ideas in their dreams. I know this is the case with me. Dreams are my primary source of new ideas. I routinely wake up with ideas for writing, for music and new projects I haven't thought of before. I treat all these ideas with great respect, honoring them as gifts, trusting in them.

In the extreme right-brain orientation of the dream state, we access the subconscious directly, which takes the form of drama, sounds, and feelings. Ideas will often be cloaked in symbolic images – this is the principle language of the dream-state. However, in its absence the importance of the left-brain becomes evident. Without the left-brain essentials of judgment, evaluation, and discrimination, we cannot determine during the dream if the ideas with which we are presented will be practical – we must bring them back to normal awareness. My habit is to simply consider all dreams important, and to review them immediately after awakening.

One of the best examples I can think of regarding dream revelation is the experience I had trying to come up with the title for my last book. I don't know if you've ever tried to title a book, but let me tell you, it's not easy. Even major publishers find it difficult. I had been seriously applying myself to finding a title for about a year. I had a notebook full of titles, and had seriously considered probably about a hundred so far – each time thinking this was the one, living with it, and then finding fault with it. It had become a major problem, and was holding up publication of the book. Then, I went away for the summer, relaxing my conscious efforts. I was camping out in my van, in the woods, when asleep in the middle of the night I saw, *Emotional Clearing*. I immediately woke up. I thought it was a good title then, and thankfully, I continued to think so. This story also illustrates that the creative subconscious has its own timetable.

## the healing process

Healing in our work means healing on a feeling level. This is where we are most blocked; where we at our point of human development are evolving, but not yet fully evolved; where we most need to learn how to handle ourselves and not abuse ourselves. Even if our primary concern is physical illness, we optimize our healing efforts by including feelings. Many authorities in the field have stated that physical illness, including heart disease and cancer, is the result of harboring unreleased feelings – the unresolved negative energy builds until it finally manifests in the physical. This accumulation of negative feeling energy is also the primary source of psychological dysfunction. Releasing these feelings is the central concern of any authentic healing modality.

Such an understanding gives rise to the need for psychology and some form of psychotherapy where the primary focus is on feelings. However, it has been my experience that meditative self-therapy can be quite effective in releasing feelings, possibly more so than most psychotherapies today, which are founded on what I consider to be outdated and outmoded concepts.

Feelings are released through awareness, acceptance, direct experience, and witnessing of them, as they are. Usually we remain reactive to our feelings – we are driven by them into all sorts of compensating behaviors instead of simply coming into the moment with the feelings. As we come into the moment, we move to a place of acceptance, where we may clearly see the feelings for the first time, where we allow ourselves to go deeper into ourselves, seeing more. If we simply sit with the feelings, not being driven by them, taking responsibility for them, just experiencing them quietly and inwardly as they are, witnessing them, the feelings will *clear*; they will release and come into balance. This is the great secret of healing.

It's the simple inner *experiencing* of feelings that accomplishes the clearing. This is because the feelings were never properly experienced when they originally occurred sometime in the past and therefore became suppressed.

How do we actually sit and experience? If we take note of what's happening inside, we may find we are driven to bring something into our lives, for example money or a relationship. And what are the feelings behind that longing? There's apt to be something like anxiety or loneliness. If we recognize this, and sit with these primary core feelings, they become released from their subconscious entrapment, and eventually cease acting on us. When this happens, we are no longer driven to seek prosperity or romance. Our needs are more balanced. It doesn't mean we will not find these things, it just means we are not compulsive about them.

It's ironic that when driven by suppressed feelings, we are unable to attain what we think we need because the feelings don't allow it. Feelings such as anxiety and loneliness actually create conditions that perpetuate themselves until we get the message that the feelings must be recognized by the conscious mind. When the conscious mind does this, and simply grants the feelings the acknowledgment they seek in the form of being experienced, the feelings are satisfied; they release, and no longer undermine our attempts to bring happiness into our lives.

If you engage in a regular sitting practice, perhaps using the simple technique we discussed in chapter two, you will find that feelings start to jump into your awareness. There are two general categories of feeling: body and emotion. Usually they are tied together and focusing on one will lead to the other.

If you first become aware of a strong body feeling, such as a physical sensation, throbbing, pressure, or pain in any part of the body, it may be assumed that something is coming forward for clearing. The body feeling may also be linked to a health condition. Staying with the feeling, *processing* it – experiencing it with complete acceptance, from the witnessing perspective – is the basic clearing/healing procedure for the condition. Allow your sensing to go to deeper, more subtle layers of the feeling. Witness without trying to change anything. Witnessing is the key that begins the natural balancing process of the body and enables you to tolerate discomfort or even pain.

As you continue to focus on the feeling, you automatically send healing energy to it, especially if you have developed this ability by having practiced with the breath. Conscious breath practice draws in *prana*, the basic healing energy of the universe that is contained in the air we breathe. This is why it is helpful to stay somewhat conscious of your breath in the background as you process the feeling.

The other general type of feeling experience that may come up as you are sitting is emotional. When this happens, recognize that suppressed emotions are surfacing for clearing. Do not become dismayed. Process them as described above. Welcome the emotions, be with them, experience them from the perspective of the witness, allow them to link to any associated life circumstance or experiences, such as childhood or other types of trauma. The emotions may be any of the typical "negative" kind with which we are all confronted: Anger, loneliness, inadequacy, sorrow, humiliation, weakness, heartbreak, loss, and also depression in general.

Do not be concerned that welcoming the feelings or ceasing to try to make them go away will cause them to increase. On the contrary, such resistance and lack of acceptance is exactly why the feelings do not clear. Understanding that the feelings need to be experienced, and accepted before they can be experienced, is the key to the true psychological process of emotional healing.

Perhaps the single most important element in the healing process is *witnessing*. To witness means to step back, to view things in a dispassionate manner, to break the unconscious identification with which we normally perceive the outer or inner world. In regard to feelings, witnessing does not mean we have no feelings. It just means we are able to witness our feelings, as they are, without being drawn into them, or without acting them out or being unconsciously motivated by them. By activating the witness, we move to a place detached from the feelings but still present with them. We turn the process over to the guidance of our higher intelligence, and healing and inner balancing occur automatically, simply by experiencing the feelings deeply.

Witnessing may be developed by deliberate sitting and practice. Just by watching the exterior or interior view with detachment, we develop the witness. The exterior is the world as it goes on around us. The interior is our reaction to it, our feelings, our thoughts, and ultimately our sense of being, itself. Witnessing is a key element in emotional clearing work. If you are not witnessing, you are usually enmeshed in the feeling, and clearing will not occur; you need to be detached. Witnessing, therefore, is instrumental in both art and personal healing and serves as a bridge to blend the two into one integrated endeavor. Witnessing also connects us to other aspects of what we may call the spiritual consciousness. As we witness, the conscious ego – the sense of "I" – is relaxed. In this expanded state, we contact the sub- and superconsciousness. We gain access to the non-ego based intelligence that will guide our work.

If you are seriously engaged in any healing work, either with or without the assistance of art, I must earnestly refer you to my *Emotional Clearing* (R. Wyler & Co. 2003) for an in-depth discussion of these basic principles as well as other indispensable subtleties of the work.

## the art process

*Art happens when feeling enters the work.*

You sit in front of the blank pad, doodling. It occurs to you that you need to get your hands a little more loose; you haven't drawn in a while. You put on a CD and sketch along with it. You feel like repeating a figure you were able to transpose from a musical phrase to a visual non-representational form. The figure starts to change as it develops. You've put your thinking mind aside, and there's a sense that the work is proceeding on its own. Then, something entirely new happens. A new shape is called forth by the presence of the first and they start interacting on the paper. You're excited. Art has happened, emerging from the subconscious.

Many times, as I go through a similar process with music, I'll find I don't have to go through a warm-up. I'll sit down at the keyboard cold and will immediately, the very first time I touch the keys, play a new phrase that instantly moves me, one which I had not been thinking of. I can feel it jumping out into consciousness, and a new composition has begun.

Or, perhaps there's been something in the back of your mind for a period of time. It's part feeling, part image, part memory, but it's not been completely clear exactly what it is. You've allowed a place for this nebulous entity. You've not demanded that it reveal its meaning immediately. You've nurtured it, and given it space to develop, to gestate. Then, one day, perhaps after months of waiting, a form appears to you. It's still incomplete, but it's enough for a beginning. You are impelled to manifest the form in the physical – you don't know exactly why, but the act of bringing the form into concrete expression gives you an intense feeling of joy. You are enchanted with the prospect of this figure revealing more of its meaning for you as it continues to evolve under your hand.

Or, you've woken that morning with an incredible vision that occurred in a dream. The feelings associated with it are so strong that you must put them down, and the right-brain mode of art appeals to you as the best way to capture the feeling: you draw, compose, write, etc.

As artists, we somehow know how to enable the creative process and let it continue into art. It starts with letting the conscious "I" set the scene and then letting "not-I" take over. Then, it ties into feeling and magic. Magic begins when we allow our consciousness to drift over into the right-brain state, with its altered sensibilities. We immerse ourselves in the medium, with our feelings accessible, open to the intercedence of higher guiding intelligence, and art happens.

Even though art has happened – *feeling has entered the work* – it may not yet tie into a healing level. We will explore the subtleties of why art does and does not heal in succeeding chapters, but we may begin the discussion here, by noting the basic conditions.

## the creative art healing process

Art heals when we allow it to *contain* the feelings we are working with. As we surrender the development of the art to the higher intelligence, we see parts of ourselves jump out into the art in the form of feelings. We don't clearly recognize these feelings at first, but as we stay with the art piece, lingering with it, contemplating it, our recognition of the feeling develops. We are able to see, *and feel*, the previously unconscious feeling that has now fully emerged through the art. Staying with the feeling as we continue to engage the art, experiencing it and integrating it through the art, is what results in clearing and wholeness.

For example, let's assume your feelings are not now settled. You have strong negative feelings towards another person for what they have appeared to have done to you – suppose you have been hurt by your lover. This situation has been sitting with you for a while, and finally it feels like it wants to get on paper. As you begin to work in your media, you have an idea in mind that you are going to express, or represent, in the art. You start with colors, and abstract or concrete images that represent *where you are now*. You find images inside and move them to the paper. You find that you want to use dark colors, you draw images that are enclosed, protected, you scribble chaotically when you think of your heart. Your intention should remain only to portray where you are now and what you are feeling now. Do not think of what needs to be done to resolve the problem. Your intent is only to remain conscious of the feeling, as reflected by and contained in the art.

You continue to make images of where you are now, over the course of a few days, weeks, or months, depending on the importance of the issue. Each time, there is a shift in the image, or in the way you have composed the scene. At the same time, each new variation of the scene represents a slightly different emphasis on your feelings. You find your feelings about this matter have changed without your trying to make them change. There has been a releasing of pain, and a spontaneous movement towards other, perhaps more objective views of the situation.

Chapters 6 and 7 expand on this theme, going into detail about optimizing the art healing process.

## finding your voice

In Santa Monica, a part of Los Angeles, there's a popular section of town called the promenade. It's a large walk-way lined with shops where street performers entertain, sometimes surrounded by large crowds. Being L.A., many of them are quite good, and they maintain a constant presence there – it seems whenever you go to the promenade, you see them.

One of these regulars is a folk singer – he performs by himself with acoustic guitar and portable PA system. What's interesting about him is that he sings and plays just like James Taylor, who was one of my favorites back in the old days. In fact, the first time I came across this performer, I heard him before I actually saw him, and for a moment I thought the real JT was making an impromptu appearance on the sidewalk.

However, while I enjoyed the performer's skill in playing and singing, I found it artistically lacking. He had not found his own voice. He was not expressing anything of himself, either with original material, nor with an individualistic interpretation of other's material. He was so into James Taylor that he had made his musical career into being a clone, of expressing someone else's soul and not his own.

We all begin our artistic efforts inspired by other artists, and we imitate them in learning our art – it's an important developmental stage. But unless we are able to put ourselves into the art and modify or synthesize styles, to come up with something original that represents us, to let the force of our own personality break through, we remain *derivative*. It's obvious who has inspired us and whose style we are copying, and the art does not contain the power it could because we are not connecting inside.

Finding your voice is an essential aspect of personal, original expression. It is important as we combine the artistic and personal growth quests because a vital element in both of them is the process of *individuation,* in which we become more and more aware of our uniqueness and cease being unconscious, conforming members of the herd.

Much of this uniqueness is of the shadow – unpleasant or painful. We have been unconsciously hiding these shadow parts because they have been unacceptable to us, based on the conditioning we have received in our culture. But as we reverse that conditioning and extend acceptance to those shadow parts, we find they are indeed essential parts of ourselves. Including them in our art is a powerful result of acceptance and also a way of making the acceptance deeper. As a result, the art grows, along with us – our voice emerges. The art becomes real and individualistic, with power and presence. It becomes a reflection of ourselves, who we are, and how much of ourselves we have discovered and integrated into our beingness.

The movement to individuation is an essential part of the spiritual path as well as the artistic. As we discover, accept and honor all those unique parts of ourselves, the "bad" and the "good," we experience growth. Paradoxically, as we expand awareness of our individuality, *consciously accepting,* we regain our connectedness and oneness on a higher level of consciousness.

Another way of looking at this is from the viewpoint of soul. Serious artists are always looking to put more soul into their work. The quest for soul can become only a stylistic search, in which we juggle appearances, shifting superficialities, but real soul is found when the work incorporates these individualistic elements of ourselves. Soul and realness on the inside shine through and the work becomes vibrant and alive.

The following exercise is an excellent way to find your voice, as well as develop the capacity for original expression.

## the NOW practice

In order to cultivate the capacity to bring the creative art experience to its fullest healing potential, I recommend that you devote time to a dedicated practice. You may think of this as a spiritual practice; that it is opening you up to levels of yourself of which you have been unaware, using art as the means. This practice directly ties into the making of art. You will find that your facility to create spontaneously will be enhanced. You will go beyond technique to include your feeling self in the work, as perhaps never before. You will find your own voice as you focus on expressing, not imitating. You will bring the experience of creating art to a new and fascinating level. You will invoke the power of *presence* and learn to let it imbue your art.

It is first necessary to understand that you will *not* be practicing technique in this exercise. Technique is what you develop when you draw from models, or when you take dance class, or practice singing scales. In a way, technique is a left-brain involvement with art. We may be active in the art arena, but we focus on skills, excluding the heart. While it's true that some skills are required in the execution of art, in our approach we put developing skills secondary to developing the aptitude required to bring feeling into the art. We allow skills – whether it's being able to draw well, move with grace, or sing on key – to develop in response to the soul's call of what is needed. The first step in performing these exercises is to shift your orientation from the left-brain intention of developing skills and technique to the right-brain non-intention of *presence*.

Sit with your chosen medium, and come into the moment. Still the mind by focusing for a few moments on the breath while breathing normally. Drop all sense of striving, of needing to accomplish anything. Become conscious of the connection between your medium and your inner awareness. Your medium is whatever form your art takes. If it's the piano, you sit at the piano, hands on the keys. If it's visual art, choose an easy medium such as drawing, but at some point you may want to open the paints each day – possibly using a cheaper grade. If you are a writer, you sit in front of your lap-top, and your expression will consist of words.

You are to allow stream of consciousness to flow through to your medium, emphasizing *feeling* – how you are feeling NOW. That's the important part. It's not about how you felt yesterday or one hour ago, it's how you are feeling NOW. Of course, how you feel NOW could be how you felt yesterday or one hour ago, so that's valid, and it's ok to re-live past events, especially if they are important, allowing the feeling to come up again, or maybe for the first time, NOW. The point is to not be in the mind, thinking about how you felt, or how you might feel in the future, but to make an opening for feeling NOW.

As the feeling comes into view, you are to allow it to be expressed without your ego participation – you are *the witness*. This means you do not choose how it will be expressed, you allow another intelligence – "not-I" – to make the choice. You surrender conscious intention. It may take you a while to get the knack of this, but don't be discouraged, you will get there.

Examples of how not-I may choose to express itself: Suppose you feel bored right now. At the piano, your left hand beats out a simple, slow, two-note phrase. And repeats three seconds later. And repeats, for the next five minutes, until something new happens, maybe with your right hand. If you are drawing with charcoal, your higher self chooses to make a simple vertical line about two inches high, but with something that looks like a bump in the middle. A few seconds later, it repeats. And repeats. If you are dancing, your left foot just goes from one spot on the floor to another while you're leaning expressively against the barre. If you're writing, you may write or type, "I'm bored," followed or not followed by any other depressing *feelings* you may have NOW. If you are an actor, you are speaking, alone in your room, repeating phrases that contain feeling. Somehow the action in each of these cases corresponds to the feeling.

If you don't like repetition, allow for continually changing expressive events that morph into each other. The value of repetition, however, is that the mind is tricked into relaxation. Even though we are trying to go beyond mind-influenced events, the mind will still try to get into the game. When it sees it does not have to work to come up with the next event because the next event is the same as the last, it goes off-duty.

What are we doing here? We are inviting the subconscious to come forward by starting quietly in stillness. In stillness, feelings that are kept suppressed below the level of consciousness will jump into awareness. These feelings, no matter what they are, must be honored by welcoming them, accepting them, being with them. By focusing only on our feelings NOW, we develop that all-important quality of *presence*. Finally, we direct the feeling to manifest in material form, experiencing the connection to the material form as it does so, allowing the material to work back on us, evoking more feeling. And in *witnessing* the experience, we set up conditions for it to move to a healing level.

After five minutes of boredom, another feeling occurs. This shifting of feelings is the essence of healing in the moment. As we stay with any one feeling or sensation, it will clear and another feeling or sensation will take its place, which may or may not be related to it. Perhaps the boredom was only a transient feeling, based on not being able to completely get into the exercise. By staying with it, it shifts to something unrelated – you remember that you have an important day ahead of you. You feel somewhat excited by this thought. The thought is valid by our NOW standards even though it concerns the future, because it is a present feeling about the future. You stay with the delightful feeling of excitement, and your expression changes automatically. If you're on the piano, both hands are now hitting the keys, but they're not playing anything you've learned or heard, they're playing some new phrase that represents your new feelings.

Soon, another feeling comes up. If you're drawing, the interesting thing here is that your hand moved to make a corresponding image on the paper before you actually connected to the feelings inside. You remember an incident from yesterday when you were frustrated and angry. The feelings come jumping into consciousness, and it becomes clear that you have been carrying them with you, unreleased. As they come forward from their suppressed place, you welcome them, feeling them, trying to put aside any blame and just coming into the moment with the feelings. These are difficult feelings, so you go back to your breath, breathing slowly, evenly, and fully into all parts of your body, especially parts where the feelings may seem to lie. You step back into the witness, distancing yourself from the feelings. You continue with the art expression, watching how the art now contains the feelings you are processing inside. If the feelings seem especially strong, you may choose to stop making the image and simply be fully with the feelings inside, closing your eyes, going within.

........................................

Other rules of the NOW practice: You are not allowed any expression you have learned, heard, read, or seen anywhere else. If you find you are falling into repeating any expression that is not original, stop and wait until something original happens.

Remember you are not trying to create any kind of finished product. You want to make images, sounds, forms, and sentences that don't look like anything but somehow contain feeling. If you

are primarily a representational artist, it may be all the more important for you to move to abstract expression. You want to scribble, to
allow the stream-of-consciousness right-brain feeling intelligence to
take over by relaxing the conscious logical left-brain mind.

Try to make the NOW practice a daily habit. A session can
last anywhere from 10 to 30 minutes. Even though the exercise may
seem trite, I can guarantee you it will loosen you up and connect
feelings and art, and will probably lead to the beginning of original
work if you are stuck. If you are a non-original artist and find the
idea of the exercise preposterous or worthless, it is likely you are
being held back by unconscious blocking. Take a chance and
commit to two weeks of daily practice and see what it can do for
you, not only in your art, but in your life.

# 5

# The
# Wounded Artist

*Why artists get stuck; Artistic depression;*
*Misusing art; The need to experience feelings*

There's a branch of psychotherapy called *art therapy*. It begins with the central assumption, as with most psychotherapeutic approaches, that what is required is the release of suppressed feelings. The participant is urged to express from within through any art form, but often painting, drawing, music, sculpture, or movement are chosen. It has been found that certain persons adapt well to this approach, finding themselves able to express feelings in the art that they could not verbally. Moreover, the actual working in the art process tends to uncover the subconscious, bringing forward suppressed material. This approach has been found to be particularly useful with children, who often lack verbal skills. Art therapy has become a bona fide type of therapy.

## art therapy

Possibly as a result of the influence of art therapy, we now see a general emphasis in consciousness circles that "art heals." The same principles apply – uncover subconscious feelings through working in the art, become more in touch with the hidden self, increase sensitivity, and above all *express yourself*. It is assumed that expression of feeling is the antidote to suppression.

All this sounds good, and to a large extent, is good. People have been helped by this approach. However, something appears to be missing. When we look at artists as a whole, especially artists who have a dedicated, ongoing relationship with their work, who are "expressing" their feelings all the time, who are not just casually experimenting with first efforts, we are presented with a startling picture. We would expect serious artists to be the most psychologically healthy group around. Instead, we find just the opposite. Artists as a group are notoriously emotionally unstable, if not dysfunctional. There has always been the allowance for the eccentric artist, but what has not been so apparent is that the eccentricity is often only the reflection of deep pain within. If art heals, what has gone wrong?

What happened to some of the greatest artists of our time – van Gogh, Poe, Schumann among others from the classical periods; William Styron, Sylvia Plath and others less well-known from contemporary times? They all experienced extreme emotional distress, some to the point of literal self-destruction.

While not all artists, well-known or not, experience severe emotional imbalance, studies have shown that the number who do is disproportionately higher than the rest of the population. There is undeniably a link between the artist and potentiality for emotional woundedness.

## manic-depressiveness

The type of distressful emotional experience that artists generally undergo is called *manic-depressive illness* or *bipolar disorder* by the psychiatric-medical establishment. At this point in time they cannot offer substantial insight into its cause, and treatment primarily relies on drugs, which I consider to be of dubious lasting value. I believe prescription drug use only serves to suppress feelings, but that they may be necessary at times to manage symptoms until other, more valid treatment can gain a foothold.

By the way, although I understand the need for a label to identify this or any syndrome, it's my opinion that implying that an *illness* is present is a disservice to the person as well as an impediment to the resolution. Illness is usually interpreted as meaning that something has been "caught;" that it is beyond the individual's control, and that the "cure" is best effected by outside intervention. Even though the motive behind the labeling of the patient's condition as illness may be well-intentioned, the subtle shift of responsibility into a blaming or victim mode – it's the illness, not me – undermines the most basic requirement of holistic healing, that of taking responsibility for oneself and one's condition.

We currently see this distortion of responsibility further encouraged by the medical establishment in the form of a multitude of "syndromes" being identified and blamed for behavior or experience, instead of simply understanding that behavioral acting-out is usually a form of defense from underlying feelings, and that painful inner dysfunction such as depression and even physical disease is the result of unconscious mismanagement of negative personal psychic energies that have been allowed to accumulate. Instead of "illness," therefore, I prefer using the term "cycle" because it implies a more natural process that results in a problem only when handled incorrectly.

In the manic-depressive cycle, we alternate between the two extremes. *Manic* is characterized as high energy, optimistic but often unrealistically so, productive but edgy and unstable, easily irritated; *depressive* is experienced painfully as the loss of energy to function and the will to go on, pessimism and despair. In manic mode, the artist creates; in depressive mode, the artist becomes self-critical. We all go through this kind of cycle; when it becomes severe enough to be threatening to our overall sense of well-being, it has reached the stage of concern.

It is noteworthy that in biographical information about artists undergoing emotional distress, they often refer to their work as having healing benefit. Whether famous or not, artists do believe they experience healing in their work and release from oppressive pain. Possibly many become artists because they find the work lessens the inner turmoil. Possibly they are given an unusual amount of pain to begin with in this life. Possibly because of their sensitivity they experience the pain of the group soul more acutely, and this leads to the inevitable depression. Possibly their purpose is to experience for the rest of the world, to express what the rest of the world can't, to be the true priests of our time.

All of this, the artist would probably agree to bear. The artist recognizes that the mission is sacred; that art takes place on a plane of being of which the average materialistically-minded citizen of today's society has no conception, and that even though it is painful and scarred, the act of creating art is one of the most transcendent, fulfilling, exhilarating experiences we can have on earth.

But we must look at this experience more closely, because if art heals, why isn't the artist healed? Why indeed, do many seem to get worse, in spite of the volume of work produced? Does art really heal?

## misusing art

Often, I would suggest that a quasi-healing effect occurs that is mistaken for true healing. To begin with, it must be recognized that the creative art process, where something is manifested from the non-linear, timeless, hidden planes of existence into the linear, time-bound reality of material consciousness, involves a unique, significant kind of stress; there is much anxiety in unearthing the subconscious. Then, the muse is not always present; the work does not seem inspired; we doubt. Anxiety-provoking, draining, demanding, producing art requires complete involvement and often sacrifice of other aspects of life.

Add to this the normal emotional pain we all carry, and we are starting the game with the table weighted against us. But we are usually not aware of this, because our first experiences with art, just as with a lover, are intoxicating. We thrill to the rush of creating, of experiencing ourselves in the creation, of feeling the high and the power that come from it. We quickly become addicted to the art experience.

What does it mean to be addicted? We are addicted to any substance, person, object, or activity when we use it to alter our feelings, *even in the name of healing*. Feelings must be experienced, just as they are, with no attempt to avoid them and with no acting-out, whatever their nature – this is the essence of the healing journey and the beginning of where we go wrong. As artists, we undergo pain from all the above sources but, having experienced the ecstasy that comes with the artistic creation, we know we can feel better, even euphoric in the elusive act of creating, so we go for it. We throw ourselves into the art experience, sometimes greedily, only in order to feel better. Essentially, we escape into the art. We escape from circumstances and harsh realities but mostly from feelings within.

And many times, it seems to work. We think we have beaten the bad feelings, but what we have done is only *suppress* them, using art as our means, even if we think we are "expressing." There is much more required to successfully clear feelings than simply their expression, whatever the form – art or otherwise. What makes this syndrome even more heart rending is that in order to be able to misuse art in this manner, we must have developed our inner, psychic skills as an artistic creator to a considerable degree.

This is what it means to engage in any activity as an *addictive compulsion*. The activity serves to push down the negative feeling, not release it, and we are left with the illusion that we have "healed" ourselves. As the suppressed feelings keep building, they return to awareness periodically with increasing intensity. We must then, like any addict, turn to our art for an even more powerful fix. We find that we oscillate between extremes of emotional experience. We dread the appearance of the suppressed negativity that disables us from creative work and leaves us depressed, and we frantically seek the creative experience itself, when we are able to finally contact the inspirational, engulfing, Bacchian force again. Before we know it, *we have created* and engaged ourselves in the destructive syndrome that is called manic-depressive illness.

We, ourselves, create the manic aspect of the high – the jittery unstableness – out of anxiety of the low. We cling anxiously and desperately to the high, trying to avoid the low at all costs. Often, we add alcohol or drugs or sex to our routine to aid in suppressing the negative feelings in hopes of getting to the transcendent creative experience, but the substance abuse only deepens the lows of the cycle with the backlash depression that comes from the stimulant's depleting the psychic energy reserves in order to produce the high. The manic-depressive cycle can be completely devastating, and is certainly present in non-artists, with whom I believe a similar dynamic will have occurred to establish the cycle, even in extreme cases.

Do you see how it works? The key elements are:

• A feeling is composed of psychic energy that must be released or else it becomes held in the subconscious, only to erupt later, demanding to be satisfied.

• These suppressed energies can build to tremendous levels and when they erupt can leave us incapacitated, unable to cope, and in the state we call depression.

• When we seek to alter these negative feelings through any means except that which results in genuine clearing, we only re-suppress the feelings, with the illusion of having healed or released them.

• We can misuse our art, our most sacred possession, as the means to suppress the feelings and bring on a cycle of highs and lows that can reach the point of becoming life-threatening.

In investigating the origins of the manic-depressive cycle, it may not be evident exactly where or how it began. The patterns may be in place from an early age, for example, with no apparent cause. The missing link here is an intelligent appreciation of the effect of what we may call previous existences on our present life experience.

Esoteric tradition supports the notion that we each have a psychological history that precedes our current conscious life. This history has contributed directly to the experiences we encounter, especially the inner, emotional experiences. In short, we carry over the suppressed emotional subconscious from one life to the next. In Eastern terms, this is referred to as *karma*. Individuals who experience emotional incapacitation with no apparent cause are only experiencing the results of previous lives. This does not mean, however, that the previous life must necessarily be recalled to clear the suppressed feelings, although this may be helpful at certain times. Working correctly with the feeling in present-time is all that is needed.

## the inner cycle

There is another way to look at the manic-depressive cycle we encounter as artists that points in the direction of balance and healing. In this holistic view, we recognize that the act of creating is essentially dualistic in nature. The ecstasy of creation is accompanied by some form of cyclical reaction – some emotional experience to complement the high. One way to account for this is from an energetic standpoint. We expend vast amounts of psychic energy in the creative moment. Recovering this energy means we must take time to regenerate, and during this period we may experience mild forms of what could be called depression. If we rebel against the "lows" of the cycle, if we don't simply take time to psychically rest, if we boost ourselves with chemicals or even the art itself, we suppress the negative and lay the ground for manic-depressive burn-out.

This was a major personal problem for me. My experience of the lows of the creative cycle was in the form of self-doubt, loneliness, and depression. I didn't understand that I had to approach these parts of my experience with the same respect and regard that I gave to the creative highs, by allowing them their right "to be," by experiencing them gently, letting them come into consciousness and clear. Instead, I suppressed them by submerging myself into more art, amplifying the cycles of highs and lows and eventually reaching the point of burn-out. This experience is what originally prompted me to personal healing and the research on feelings integration that resulted in my previous book.

Now, I understand that in order to handle the creative cycle, I must allow all aspects of it to come forth into consciousness as I engage in making art, and that I must not be attached to any particular one. When the highs come, I welcome them, I enjoy them, but not out of any compulsive need to stay in the high because I am avoiding any other part of life. When the highs have expended themselves and the negative side of the cycle is coming forward, I welcome it too with unconditional acceptance as integral to the whole, sitting with it, being with it, witnessing and experiencing it.

I believe we should view the manic-depressive cycle as an inherent part of the art-making process – a concept we will expand later as we discuss the three stages of art – and definitely not as an illness. We will learn to *integrate* the cycle and make both aspects a positive experience instead of being thrown by the emergence of the inevitable low. The cycle only becomes a problem when mismanaged, when the low is suppressed and allowed to build instead of being experienced and brought into balance.

Understanding that the creative high results in the creative low, which again prepares us for the high, greatly helps to get through the cycle. The high, the manic part, is associated with the elation we experience in the art when certain stages are achieved. The low follows because the high needs to be balanced – we need to become grounded once again. We cannot stay in the high because of its very nature and the current limits of our consciousness. The low brings with it the tendency towards depression and the potential for the self-critical voice that can be such a difficult part of the art process. The self-criticism is not a vicious part of ourselves that needs to be eliminated, but is how we experience the low when it remains unintegrated.

## experience, not expression

Let's return to the question of why artists don't heal. Even if we are not abusing our art as a means to mood-alter, how is it possible to engage, even fiercely, in the expression of feelings and still be wounded? Why don't artists heal? What essential element in the making of art has been overlooked or misunderstood?

The notion that "expression" of a feeling is what's needed to release it from its suppressed place in the subconscious is a concept that was at one time, and may still be, the prevalent attitude about feelings work held by the psychological establishment. It is thought you must get rid of the feeling and "get it off your chest." It is often unclear what "expressing it" is supposed to mean, except that it is the presumed opposite to keeping the feeling "in," where it will build and fester.

It is possible to understand the logic of this, and to even agree that there is some validity to it, because when we express – such as in verbalizing a hidden feeling – we do experience a certain movement of the trapped energy and a sense of relief. However, it is my belief and experience, both personal and professional, that the ultimate healing benefit obtained from expression is relatively ineffectual, and that this is one of the reasons that psychotherapy, including art therapy, based on the paradigm of expression has proven to be limiting. Indiscriminate expression can often cause additional problems as well; for example, if we blamefully express our feelings to another in the unenlightened belief that they are responsible for our experience.

How do we actually clear feelings and avoid their build-up through suppression? How do we avoid the trap of using our art as a suppressive mechanism? The key principle of inner emotional healing is that

*Experience of a feeling, not expression, is the resolution to suppression.*

This is true whether we are working in the arts as a healing medium or with any other type of therapy. Expression of a feeling is not the same as experience of it. Expression may include experience, but may also hinder it – we look outward instead of inward. This is a principle we must understand thoroughly as artists, especially when we seek to include a healing dimension in our work. If expression of a feeling, meaning portrayal of it in an art form, were all that were needed, all artists would be healed or at least would have a strong sense of moving in that direction, and this is not the case. Grasping at the illusion of exorcising pain through its expression in the art, we fall harder into the inevitable depression when the pain remains.

Expression of a painful feeling, whether verbal or artistic, only begins the process of healing and release – more is needed to complete it. The capacity for artistic expression increases our awareness of our feelings, our sensitivity, our intuition, our ability to articulate the feeling, and eventually our awareness of the inner blocking which prevents direct experience of the feeling, but it is the deep inner experiencing that ultimately releases the feeling. Not being fully experienced is what suppressed the feeling in the first place.

Actually, it is unnecessary to "express" outwardly in any art or verbal form to oneself, one's therapist, or another person if one can connect deeply and directly to the feeling experience within. The only expression required is expression of the feeling *into consciousness, with complete acceptance*, and this may be done for the most violent feelings while sitting quietly, which I believe is the optimal condition for feeling release.

Outward expression can be misused, and can impede the inner experiencing and eventual clearing of feelings and healing of self. If, as an artist, you have reached a certain level of competence and sensitivity in working with feelings, and you are clearly aware of a certain feeling or psychological pattern within yourself but you continue to simply "express" the feeling in your work, you are likely to be expressing when you should be feeling. You need to move on, you are caught in a loop. There's a subtle, but all important difference here. The art becomes used as a means to avoid authentic inner feeling. The suppression is continued, and the art does not heal.

This, then, is the crucial factor in whether art has healing value: Do you allow yourself to move deeply into the feelings that are roused from the subconscious by the process of making the art? If not, no matter what your level of technical expertise, you will not reach the healing level. You either escape into the art, where you may not allow your real feelings to be known, or if you are more astute about your emotional self and try to portray your real feelings in the art you still do not find the release you are seeking because you don't move effectively into feeling.

Our attitude towards feelings is crucial in setting up the proper mental/psychic environment that will allow them to clear. Acting on the impulse to get rid of the feeling is what keeps it locked within, unable to release. We think if we can transfer the feeling to the art, we won't have to feel it. It's this inner rejection of the feeling that makes us unable to move to a place of being able to experience it, as must be done, in order to clear the energy.

What is needed is to experience it with complete acceptance, and not to do so as a means to get rid of it. The impulse to get rid of the feeling, to get it off your chest, whether by verbally attacking someone, or discussing quietly how someone else is to blame for your feelings, or trying to get it out by "expressing" it in an art piece is all the same. The motive *to get rid of* dooms the releasing of the feeling on deep levels. If you keep constructing art pieces with the intention of expressing the feeling in order get rid of it, your result will not be achieved.

## artistic depression

Depression is the condition of depletion of inner psychic energy – the energy we use to think, feel, and generally function as human beings. Depletion may result from overwork, stress, worry, poor nutrition; excessive smoking, alcohol, drugs, or sex; negative relationships; and any other way that drains energy. Although depression is largely the experience of energetic depletion and not a true emotion, I believe it can be suppressed and stored just as an emotion. The depletion keeps getting bigger.

When our energy is drained, we don't have the fortitude to deal with the most trivial problem, and we think we are depressed because of the problem. The real problem is the condition of our energy. Often, we throw ourselves back into the very activity responsible for our condition in a reckless effort to feel better instead of working intelligently with the depression, and we become caught in addiction and the manic-depressive cycle.

The primary drain on our psychic energy resources, however – of which we are not usually aware – is the energy expended to keep feelings suppressed, or blocked, in the subconscious. The act of suppression itself consumes a huge amount of energy, and we often develop addictions only in order to supply this. We all misuse our energy to a certain extent in unconscious blocking – it is part of the human condition at this stage of evolution, and we all could have much more energy at our disposal if we entered upon a regular process of uncovering and releasing these trapped feelings. But if depression is chronic and severe, it generally means we are carrying a large amount of negative feelings in the subconscious, and that we are engaging in a great deal of suppression to keep them there.

There is no one particular feeling common to all individuals that is kept suppressed and lurks behind the depression. The feelings can be any of the usual or unusual negative inner feelings: anger, grief, defeat, heartbreak, rejection, frustration, anxiety, worthlessness, and so on. The feelings are likely to be a mixture of what could be called existential feelings with more personal ones. "Existential" refers to feelings deriving directly from the archetypal human condition – the universal experience that we as a collective must resolve and with which the artist works.

In working with depression, therefore, after covering preliminary bases concerning nutrition, rest, and lifestyle, we expect there will be a considerable amount of emotional clearing work to be done. Clearing feelings behind the depression is the primary strategy for treating the depression. As feelings are cleared, it will become relatively easy to drop the addictive behavior that is perceived as necessary to keep feelings in check.

Artists may be especially susceptible to depression because of their closeness to the dark side of experience, to which they are drawn as part of their work – the work of revealing the subconscious shadow, reclaiming lost parts, and moving towards wholeness, which they perform for themselves as well as the collective. These raw and wild energies can get out of control and become overwhelming and will often tempt the artist into suppressing them in any number of ways such as using the art as an escape, alcohol/drug/sex abuse, self-criticism, or any means that negates an authentic feeling stance. A negative pattern of responding to the feelings is established and depression is inevitable. The artist needs, perhaps more than most people, tools to work with and to manage feelings. Even though the feelings may be powerful – especially when they result from tapping into the archetypal collective – they will still respond to the techniques of emotional processing that we are exploring in this book.

I remember reading William Styron's courageous and poignant story of his encounter with depression, *Darkness Visible*, when it came out in the late eighties. I remember being angry that he had not been able to find a medical or psychological advisor who could explain to him the nature of his experience so he could understand what was happening. Styron relates that, after a lifetime of use, he one day found that his body would violently refuse to assimilate any amount of alcohol, and he was thrown into a deep, unprecedented depression. The sudden intolerance of the alcohol is, in itself, interesting from a healing perspective. We could probably find medical reasons for it but we could also, and just as credibly to me, suggest that some unconscious intelligence was at work, finally saying "enough" – the self-destructive cycle must end now.

All drug use, including alcohol, affects a suppression of undesired feelings. The mood is altered, the painful feelings seem to go away, the creative muse may speak, but at the cost of the continuing build-up of the suppressed negative feelings. With the absence of alcohol, Styron's accustomed means to suppress the negativity that had accumulated over the years was no longer available. Confrontation with this stored body of negativity is likely to have resulted in a reaction similar to shock or trauma. Overwhelm may have occurred, which will often lead to *disassociation*. In this automatic defense mechanism, the ego, the seat of awareness, no longer connects to the feeling self, and confusion and despondency follow. Depression sets in, compounded by the instinctive reaction to push the negativity away by willful suppression – to do with the mind what the alcohol had previously accomplished. This suppressive act of the mind drains large quantities of psychic energy, adding to the inner depletion.

In approaching such a challenging situation we would start with the understanding that misuse of alcohol, though traditional among artists and especially writers, serves as a suppressive mechanism to negative feelings – some unique to the artist, some just from ordinary life. The unreleased feelings keep building in the subconscious, contributing to the depression and inviting further substance abuse as a means to suppress them. This manner of managing experience results in the manic-depressive cycle – escaping from the low by means of the mood-altering substance and the art high, falling into the low because of the exhaustion of psychic reserves, and starting all over again.

## handling depression

If you are experiencing significant depression, you need to enter upon a dedicated program, either by yourself or with help. Adequately discussing such a program is beyond the scope of this book; however, I have been alluding to its important elements, and will try to summarize them here:

Working with the experience of depression itself, even though it is largely the result of suppression and not a "real" feeling, may proceed in exactly the same way as with any other emotional feeling. Recognize that depression is an energetic condition. Feel it, witness it as an energetic experience. Detach and break your identification with it; accept and watch. Use the powerful tools of breathwork and bodywork. If you are working alone, it can be helpful to be linked to a healing force such as a group, a spiritual master, or a universal, natural energy source.

As you sit with depression, the feelings behind it that have been suppressed and have accumulated will eventually come into awareness to be processed in the same way. Do not think you are getting worse when this happens. Recognize that the subconscious is being revealed to be healed. Trust that you are being guided and protected by the higher self. Many feelings – simple and basic feelings like fear, anxiety, anger, loneliness, jealousy, sexual compulsiveness – are likely to be already conscious, waiting to be engaged properly so they can be cleared. If you work with them, you will be led to deeper core feelings, issues, and patterns that will ultimately result in complete healing and balance. Including art in your process will add another vital dimension to the healing potential.

If you are conscious of only the depression and not any negative feelings in particular, then you are in a repressed condition – without awareness – and working to uncover and release the feelings is even more urgent. The repressed feelings attract adversity, failure, addictions, and ultimately result in break-down of the physical body.

As feelings behind the depression are cleared, balance will be restored. In cases of severe manic-depressiveness, we would expect the healing period to be substantial; a lifetime of mismanagement of feelings cannot be reversed overnight. On the other hand, when starting serious therapy, it's possible to experience meaningful catharsis immediately. These initial moments of release are experienced as a true blessing, and we are substantially encouraged. We find we are able to be at peace with the journey itself.

If depression is severe, it can be helpful to work with a therapist. Judicious use of prescription drugs might be called for as a means to help manage feelings as an adjunct to therapy, but therapy should be the central means through which healing occurs. The genuine emotional supportiveness of a good therapist – someone who is able to make an energetic link with the client and is not just dispensing drugs – can do a great deal to enable the client to proceed through the therapy period without or with minimal drugs.

There is no question in my mind that it is the buildup of suppressed feelings that results in the chronic depressed and manic-depressive condition. Depression is not a disease we catch, even in its most severe forms. It is not genetically acquired, even though persons who are susceptible to it may tend to be attracted to one another and may incarnate together in family groups. Depression is the result of ignorance and mismanagement of experience. We fall into a pattern of suppressing feelings instead of allowing them to release, resulting in addictive tendencies and the manic-depressive experience.

# part 2

Making Art With Feeling

# 6

# Making Art

*Finding ourselves in the art; Projection;*
*The movement to wholeness;*
*Product and process art; Darkness in art*

What do we really do when we create art? How can the experience
be so powerful, in both a positive and negative sense? What draws
us in so intensely? In order to address these questions, we must look
more closely into the psychological dynamics of art-making, and in
particular to how the phenomenon known as *projection* operates
within the artistic experience.

We began a discussion of projection in chapter two, when we
noted that as experiencers of art, we tend to create our own
meaning. The art we view may be assumed to be a "screen" of sorts,
which serves as a means for us to become aware of – to project – the
inner, subconscious contents of our minds.

The most common way in which the subconscious first
becomes known is through feeling. If we accept whatever our
feeling may be as we engage the art, taking responsibility for it
without acting it out, witnessing it, we may move through the
feeling – where we were likely to have been stuck – to a higher,
more liberated experience of ourselves. In using art in this manner,
it takes on its healing benefit, becoming an accelerated microcosm

of life, where we unwittingly engage in exactly the same process, projecting onto other people and circumstances, creating our own meaning.

It is important to understand that projection is an unconscious, natural process. It is not desirable or possible to stop it – it is a central way we grow. We make best use of it when we understand how it works, and then work with it. Whenever we experience some emotionally meaningful event, it is likely we have contributed to it substantially through our projecting. If we recognize that we are projecting, we take the first crucial step. We become conscious.

Our most common experiences with projection will involve objects that are not normally considered to be art. For example, walking on a dark, lonely road at night, you become unusually frightened even though you know there is nothing to harm you; you project your fear. When the inclination and capacity to project onto art is developed, a similar process takes place. You may see a painting or film, or read a description of a dark, lonely road. If your empathic powers are strong, you may have the same feelings you had on the actual road. At the same time, you know that your interaction with the art is not "real," and you are delighted with being stimulated and tricked.

As the art we engage becomes more varied and complex, greater range is available for our projections, and we can go to deeper levels within ourselves. It is important to allow for and even to seek out these types of experiences, and to see them for what they are – a means for the subconscious to clear itself – and to use them productively.

## artistic projection

Artistic projection is the foundation of the creative art experience. Until projection occurs, the art we make has no real meaning or power for us.

*It is only when projection occurs - when subconscious feeling has entered the work - that the work comes alive. The work comes alive only when projection has occurred.*

You find a piece of driftwood on the beach. It intrigues you. It becomes a wonderful, graceful, abstract representation for you of something, but you don't know what. You linger with the object, you take it home, you place it carefully on a table, you spend time with it, admiring it. You somehow feel more at peace and less in need. You feel more whole within yourself. This delightful fascination is the signal that you have entered into an *artistic projection* with the object – you have entered the magical realm of art.

The exact nature of the relationship is not yet known, but it is quite likely that if you continue to contemplate the object, meaning you sit with it, observe it, admire it, feel your relationship with it as far as is known and let it affect you, you will eventually see what it holds for you. You see that the driftwood represents that hidden part of you that longs to be free and spontaneous, symbolized by the random, free-form shape that has become smooth and graceful by simply allowing itself to be worked on by the elements; and by the history of the piece, as it has been romantically carried from distant parts of the world by the sea with no plan but has ended up with you.

As you continue to be with the object, you realize you are attracted to these qualities – the qualities you are projecting –

because they are absent in your life. You are led to other feelings, feelings of being held-down and restricted, and associated circumstances of which you were not particularly aware. What has been revealed to you through sitting with the object are aspects of yourself that were previously unknown and suppressed. These feelings can now be productively integrated by processing them – accepting, experiencing, and witnessing them – in order to clear them and the circumstances, and the art itself can further be used to assist in the integration, by continuing to sit with it. Note that if you attempt to change the circumstances that appear to be holding you down without first clearing the feelings within, you are likely to be unsuccessful. It's the suppressed feelings that attract the circumstances, not the other way around.

This is the nature of artistic projection. At a certain point, we have had enough experiences with either "found objects" or other people's art and are compelled to produce our own images, enabling us to move to a deeper, more direct representation of the subconscious. We dabble for a while with paint, or play for a while with a few chords, but then the fascination hits, signaling the occurrence of an artistic projection. An image has emerged from the subconscious, mirroring a *lost part* of ourselves that needs to come into the light, a part that is cut-off and unknown but now symbolized and reflected by the art, and known to us through feeling. The lost part of ourselves is seen as an *other*, as part of the art, but because we *identify* with it as we perceive it projected in the art, we momentarily experience a greater level of the wholeness towards which we are unconsciously striving so intensely as human beings.

The *projection, recognition, and identification* with the cut-off aspect of ourselves first takes place on an *unconscious* level, though not as unconscious as before the process began. The aspect is emerging, and we are only beginning to get a glimpse. We do not yet know why we are attracted so strongly; we just know that we are. In time, the nature of the attraction will be fully revealed.

## the movement to wholeness

Being brought into contact with lost parts of ourselves results in a greater sense of inner wholeness. We have been unconsciously cut off from these lost parts, but now that they have been brought to our attention, we become aware of just how much we have been lacking. The reunion with cut-off parts of ourselves is intrinsically joyful, fulfilling, and emotional. The drive towards wholeness is our strongest impulse; it is our basic spiritual need. The satisfaction of this need is what we mean by happiness.

It is the experience of reunion that gives meaning and power to the artistic encounter. As we find those previously cut-off parts of ourselves emerging in the art under our hand, we are mesmerized and elated. We unconsciously recognize ourselves, we move towards wholeness, and we feel the incredible joy and satisfaction that accompanies it. This is why we become artists. It is what makes the experience of making art so captivating and transcendental.

Even though the experience of wholeness is temporary when it takes place within projection, it is still emotionally meaningful. Other steps will follow in which we naturally *withdraw* our projection from the object, and see clearly that the qualities we now sense to be part of the art are really part of ourselves, just hidden because of our suppression or our natural unfolding of consciousness as we progress in our evolution. Then, we experience a final and authentic reunion with this aspect of the hidden self, and the particular growth cycle is completed.

It's important to have a full understanding of these cut-off parts of ourselves that enter the art. As they remain trapped in the subconscious, we experience the limitation of the human condition. The parts themselves are bursting to come forward into consciousness. They have an elementary form of intelligence and willfulness that propels them to attach to appropriate objects of projection – objects that will carry that kind of feeling. We don't really have any conscious control over exactly what type of projection and resultant animation will occur. However, this is part of the fun. We surrender to the wisdom of the subconscious, and let it bring forth what it deems most appropriate.

These suppressed aspects of ourselves that enter our art through projection are of two types: positive and negative. It may be assumed that negative aspects derive primarily from subconscious shadow material, largely of our own making, but with the possibility that some may have collective or archetypal or some sort of "original sin" derivation. This shadow material is primarily composed of painful feelings that have remained unfelt and therefore undischarged, such as sadness or helplessness. "Negative" projections are therefore experienced as uncomfortable or painful.

For example, if you are watching a film and especially dislike a certain character, it is likely a negative projection has occurred. You perceive a suppressed quality of your own transferred unconsciously to the character. Since we essentially condemn a quality when we suppress it within ourselves, we tend to transfer that condemnation to the perceived projected quality as well as the object on which we are projecting. The condemnation results in our getting upset or annoyed. We are repelled by the qualities we see in the character.

Most difficult projections will be concerned with emotional feelings. If you have a lot of suppressed anger inside, you will be sensitive to anger or violence portrayed in the film. You may tend to be impatient with any display of anger. You may even see anger where there is none, your perception colored by inner layers of suppressed and projected feeling. If you have suppressed the feeling of weakness, you may tend to despise any character who displays weakness. If you have suppressed the feeling of hatred, you may condemn, perhaps condescendingly, anyone who exhibits hatred. If you have condemned sexuality within yourself you may be uncomfortable or even despise others when you perceive it in them, especially if they appear to be giving it uninhibited expression.

At the same time, however, another consequence of carrying suppressed feelings is a fascination with them when we perceive them projected, and being drawn to them in an attempt to find wholeness and to unite with what is lacking in ourselves. So while we disapprove of anger, we are mesmerized by it. We are attracted to and can even be in awe of those who seem to be able to freely express their anger, inviting them into our lives even though we may understand that they are by no means well-adjusted and that associating with them is self-destructive. We might even erroneously think their ability to demonstrate anger is a kind of strength. Similarly, we abhor weakness, but root for the underdog. We self-righteously condemn hatred, but thrill in seeing acts of hatred enacted. We consider sexuality a sin, but are drawn into dark, secret tunnels of acting-out unfulfilled passions.

Positive cut-off parts of ourselves may be considered to have been suppressed along with painful shadow feelings. The blocking we create to shield us from the negative also blocks the positive, and that's why as we release the negative, we enjoy spontaneous access to more positive feelings, qualities, abilities and experiences. This inner blocking of the negative is the main reason creativity becomes limited.

When the positive is blocked, we tend to project the positive as well as the negative onto other people or art. Not being in touch with our love, we think we see it outside ourselves, and we must possess the object to regain our wholeness. For example, in a romantic projection, harmonious inner aspects of ourselves, yet to be actualized, are seen in the other. A man may be attracted to tenderness, charm, softness, intuitiveness, beauty and nurturing qualities in a woman – qualities from which he is cut off within himself. A woman may be attracted to strength, intelligence, power, cleverness and ability in a man – qualities from which she is presently cut off in herself. If there's also a sexual attraction between them, we have what we call romantic love. Both are attracted to aspects of themselves yet to be activated. In the attraction, they each become more whole, and the sense of incompleteness, or emptiness, is assuaged, at least temporarily.

## making art

As we enter the creative process more fully, we begin to work in various media. We paint, we write, we compose, we sculpt. We invite the subconscious to come forward in the form of projection. We experience the satisfaction inherent in any creative activity, whether it is making a painting or building a house or cooking a meal. However, as we have touched upon, not all creative activity is art. Creative activity that does not include the projection process may be called "craft." Certainly much skill may be applied in the creation of a beautiful object, but art happens when subconscious feeling enters the work; when the steps of unconscious *projection, recognition, and identification* have occurred. Then, we open the door to the deep, hidden self and the essence of art.

Art is the intersection of feeling and matter; that place between the moon and the walking; the language of the magical realm. "Feelings" include emotions, desires, needs, impulses, moods, intuitions, pain, joy and in general any of the infinite levels of human beingness including the universal archetypes. When any of these elements of spirit enter into a material object or composition, which occurs primarily through artistic projection, we have created art. We have infused the object with psychic life, giving birth to a magical entity with, to a considerable extent, an independent existence. We, or anyone else, may enter into relationship with it, interact with it, and be influenced by it. If we impart feeling into matter with a developed sense of esthetics, we produce a powerful art statement that will entice us with its beauty and presence, opening us to the dramatic presentation of the human experience.

We make art as a spiritual discipline and celebration – a means to advance our personal and collective unfolding evolution of consciousness. More specifically, we make art for two purposes: to know a part of ourselves better, or to make the unknown known. We call these two types of art *product* and *process*. Product art is *representative*. It shows and explores further what is known. Process art is *evocative*. It invites the unknown to come forward. In practice, both types may blend. We may start with a product approach and glide into process, but it's important to understand the potentials and limitations of both modes in order to be able to apply either as may be appropriate, and not to avoid any one mode because of lack of familiarity.

## product portrayal of feeling

In making art that is concerned with feeling, our first attempts are usually to *illustrate* or *communicate* a *known* feeling. We may try to portray our inner experience, as if we are telling it to another. We put our sadness into a song or our anger into a painting. This, in its most basic form, is the *art therapy* approach. This can be an important step. For those who are deeply repressed, just being able to look in the direction of feelings is therapeutic. Portraying an experience in any art form shows that sensitivity to feelings is developing. But it is important to understand that if our level of expression does not go beyond this point, it is unlikely that we will experience significant healing benefit from our art. We may even be seduced by the high of the creative act itself, and not realize that we are not fulfilling the therapeutic purpose of engaging in the art, which is to release feelings.

We do not experience growth by merely portraying the known, even when we are trying to "express" a feeling. We usually hope that by illustrating a feeling faithfully in the art, we will exorcise it, that the feeling will enter the art and leave us. This kind of art is sometimes called "scapegoat" art. The art may then even be destroyed, with the hope that the transferred feeling will also disappear. The operation is similar to primitive black magic rites where talismans are imbued with undesirable qualities and then disposed of. Reports can be found about these rites that might seem to confirm their effectiveness; however, such results are illusory. Even though short-term energetic manipulations are possible, the eventual result is only further build-up of the subconscious reservoir of suppressed negativity and an increased need to defend against the build-up.

Product art is often associated with a "message" – what is the artist telling us? We think that art must have a point when we come at it from the left-brain. But art that contains a preconceived message is of questionable value as art. It is basically only a lecture with an esthetic presentation – a means to persuade others to a point of view – and quickly becomes boring. Art intended in this sense will not contain the timeless vitality that good art has.

## product containment of feeling

In order for authentic feeling to be evoked and for art to be healing in product mode, we have to move to a different relationship with the art. We may start with a product illustration of feelings, by representing where we are now. But as we keep working with the images, whatever our media, we allow for a shift in the way we interact with the art. Instead of working with the intention of getting rid of a feeling, we work with the intention of *being with* the feeling, and of *experiencing* it through the art.

*We allow the art to contain the feeling for us.*

This crucial shift of purpose aligns art with emotional healing work. Entering the art, which we are simultaneously producing, with the sense of a participant, with the sense that this is happening NOW, that I am not merely illustrating what may have happened in the past, allows the *realness* - the presence - to enter the art that is so crucial in making it come alive, and for authentic healing and energetic shifting to occur. In practical terms, if we are working with an event of the past, we *relive* the event as we make the art. As we go through the steps of what happened, putting those feelings into material expression, we both contain the feelings and distance ourselves from them. We are with the feelings, but witnessing them.

It's important to distinguish between portrayal and containment of feeling. In portrayal, the artist starts with an awareness of the feeling that will be depicted. The intention, which may be unconscious, is to get rid of the uncomfortable feeling. But, for reasons we may not entirely understand, the portrayal of the feeling has a sense of self-consciousness about it, a sense of self-indulgence. It is being portrayed as means to an end. It is almost or blatantly a cry for attention: look at my pain. It is a self-centered *illustration* of a feeling, but the work does not *contain* the feeling. There is no inherent power that might draw us to participate in the creation as viewers.

Contrastingly, in containment, the feeling is not illustrated in order to get rid of it. It might be hoped by the artist that this would occur at some point, but this is not the purpose of the work. Indeed, the work has no ulterior purpose, except *to hold the feelings so that the artist may experience them through the work*. The artist uses the art to *be with* the feelings. The work *embodies* the feelings, and is not merely telling about them. In doing so, the work invites the archetypes to enter – it acquires universal significance – and takes on power, realness, and presence, becoming something with which everyone can identify and experience. The art becomes magical.

As you continue working in product/containment, your mode may shift to process. This means that new feelings will emerge through the work – feelings of which you were not aware. You may have been sad to start with, without knowing why you were sad. As you allow the art to shape itself you might see, for example, images of being hungry. You soon realize it's an emotional hunger. You are sad because of an absence of nurturing in your life; you don't feel nurtured by people around you, and you don't nurture them. You mourn the lack of this quality. You make another picture and through the image come into contact with the suppressed anger previously buried under the sadness and depression that resulted from the frustrated need for emotional nurturing. You may have flashbacks to earlier times when you painfully experienced the absence of nurturing, such as childhood.

These are the kinds of feelings that are to be consciously integrated through the art. You continue to just *be with* the feelings, experiencing, witnessing, as they embody themselves in image after image, expending their energy. You then experience spontaneous, unexpected growth. You are then able to rationally explore how these needs may be addressed in present close relationships.

You may notice that some degree of psychological facility is required to recognize and make your way through the kinds of feelings that are encountered when the subconscious is evoked. If you have been involved with inner work over the years, this will be of great advantage. This facility can be acquired through therapy, workshops, reading, or talking with knowledgeable friends.

## process art

*Process art* is a term used in the art field to describe a particular approach to making art. In process art, we usually do not start with the intention to work with any particular feeling. In fact, feelings are usually stuck in the subconscious and are not known, except for possibly some superficial, first-level feelings that might, or might not, lead to significant deeper waters with a product/containment approach. Instead, we enter the flow of the subconscious, following what *attracts* us, allowing it to unfold on its own.

The art work itself will definitely show a difference with this kind of orientation. When portrayed as product, art tends to be sterile because no life has been captured. What has been represented is an intellectual conception, possibly the intellectual conception of a feeling. In process, we enter the river of the subconscious, where life is happening NOW, in this moment. Working without intention to portray any particular image, we allow ourselves to be guided, according to what attracts us. The work unfolds itself, in either representative or abstract form, and brings to light rich gifts of the subconscious. The work shows a greater sense of connection. It goes beyond being intellectual to being authentic.

Authenticity is the subtle but essential element in any art that is perceived by the sensitive viewer and enables the art to come alive. Because life has been allowed to enter the art and because the art has a powerful sense of *realness* and *presence*, another person may engage it. The art will reach out and pull them in. If the work is only intellectual, if it only illustrates, even when concerned with important personal feelings, there will be no power in the art to move the viewer.

What is it exactly that goes into the art to give it this essential authentic realness and presence, and how do we provide it? For me, the first requirement is *a sense of being in the moment as the art is created* – of seeing the art always as new, letting the art act on us, evoking responses from the subconscious in the form of genuine feelings that will magically find their way into embodiment, letting ourselves be guided and opening to the emergence of the unknown in the art. This does not mean, by the way, that feelings or emotions as we normally think of them need be in ostentatious display for an art piece to contain presence. Great presence can be evoked simply by being.

A good example of the importance of coming into the moment within the art experience can be seen in the field of acting. The actor must respond spontaneously to the drama as if encountering it for the first time. We have all seen actors who have not developed their skill to this level. It is apparent that they are *expecting*, that they know what is coming, that they are prepared to react, that they are thinking and have their lines ready, that they are acting and not inter-acting. They are not in the moment. The performance lacks realness, presence, soulfulness, sensitivity – those magical qualities that give power to the work. In contrast, the actor who has mastered the skill of being in the moment appears totally real and believable, and transmits the power that moves us. But in order to appear spontaneous, the actor must actually be spontaneous. This occurs with movement into the moment.

The same principle can be applied to any art. Any performance, such as music or dance, must be engaged in the moment – not only when performing for others, but when we are composing in private – in order to allow realness to enter and the new to come forward. If we are not in the moment with a visual art composition as it evolves before us, continually seeing it as new, we lose the connection to realness. We are thinking about what to do next, instead of just letting it happen and watching as a witness. In writing, especially when editing, the greatest skill is to be able to clear the mind, to come into the moment, and see the page as if for the first time, letting the work act on us as it will on a reader new to it.

The capacity to work in the moment is developed as we advance on our personal path. It is essentially a spiritual quality. In this context, spirituality might be defined as the opening of consciousness through movement into the self. Perhaps that is why so often the spiritual and artistic paths coincide. In practical terms, the capacity to be in the moment is developed as we practice witnessing.

The key to deep process work, whether in psychotherapy or the arts, is to hand over direction to this other guiding force, however we may conceive of or experience it. This guiding force operates by revealing to us various qualities and components that we will want to include in our art because *it pleases us*. Who or what is this guiding force? It is composed of our shadow subconscious, which is trying to come forward into awareness to be released, and which will impel us to include dark elements in the work; and that superconscious part of ourselves, which some may think of as a power outside ourselves, which will urge us to include elements of light and love. When we hand over control to these forces, the work becomes inspired. We recognize that it is not our conscious ego-mind that is coming up with the artistic manifestation. Some other guidance is surely at hand.

Sometimes we don't at first see the significance between parts of the art piece as it is forming when guided by the unseen intelligence. Elements will seem out of place, awkward, wrong, like mistakes. If we learn to trust, we often see later that the apparent incongruities come together in a way we could not have foreseen or planned. We are presented with the unconscious recognition of the hidden, split-off, undeveloped parts of ourselves. We thrill to the emergence of these aspects in the art as they take shape before us. Trusting in guidance, we are rewarded.

## interpretation

Process art is characterized by the postponing of interpretation, possibly indefinitely. The notion that art must be interpreted to be of value comes directly from the early psychoanalytic, scientific reliance on the rational mind. This approach holds that inner healing must be accomplished through analysis: Finding the original "cause" of the current condition, usually presumed to be in early childhood; understanding how the cause resulted in a "complex" – a dysfunctional pattern that was adopted unconsciously in order to compensate for the traumatic psychic injury; and then "intervening" – an action by the therapist designed to disrupt the pattern. This kind of attack on the problem is typical of the intrusive, left-brain approach, where intellect rules.

Reliance on the left-brain has much to do with the alienation that we as a society currently experience between each other and within ourselves. In believing that we can solve all problems logically, we have cut ourselves off from the right-brain, intuitive, nurturing side of ourselves that connects us to the earth, the feminine, the mystery of creation and the ultimate healing that we seek. When we attempt to interpret art to find out "what it means," we turn away from this magical realm. Indeed, the idea that art has to mean anything is a left-brain distortion and expectation.

Moreover, if we interpret the art we are creating, we usually do so prematurely, before the art has reached the point where it might be said to be a full representation of any subconscious condition. We are meddlesome with our interpretation. We do not allow the art to work on us as it must. Process art should not be seen primarily as a statement. Instead, it becomes an extension of one's inner process; it *is* one's inner process. It is oneself, cloaked in metaphor, hidden behind a veil. If we go up to it and brazenly demand that it reveal itself, it will flee and the magical state will be lost.

If we are not to intellectually interpret, how is the art to be of value? We must approach the art carefully and quietly, and wait for it to reveal itself through *feeling*, not intellect. We must contemplate the art as we are creating it. To contemplate means to be with, to relax with, to notice, to admire, to enjoy. Just being able to extend this kind of attention to any object represents a developed consciousness. Through contemplation, we invite the art to show itself as ourselves. Feelings will emerge. Memories may be stirred of times when strong feelings were present but were suppressed. Or, we may just linger with present feelings that are evoked, which are essentially the same feelings that were suppressed in the past, now projected. Either way is satisfactory to effect emotional release. There is no imperative need to go back to some past episode.

## positive process

Deep process work means we become aware of hidden parts of ourselves – not only feelings, but also qualities that have become lost. One of the classic artists of our time who comes to mind relative to the yearning for freedom I have mentioned is Jack Kerouac. I remember reading his books when I was young and being enamored by all his central characters, who are rebellious, free-spirited, who drive wildly and romantically across the country, unbound by the conventions of job, responsibility, or family. In them, I found encouragement to follow my own impulses to break free. I imagined Kerouac himself to be a fierce, wild personification of these qualities and regarded him as a hero. I was disappointed to later learn from his biography (*Kerouac* by Ann Charters, Warner 1974, New York) that Kerouac the man was nothing like his characters – a syndrome quite common among artists, I now understand. He lived most of his life in his mother's house, unable to support himself, an alcoholic. His books represented only his unrealized desires.

Intense longing for rebellious freedom is symptomatic of a deeper frustration. The biography does not specifically explore this frustration, but we could speculate that Kerouac might have encountered unusual restriction at some point in his past, possibly inflicted by a father or other authority figure. Or perhaps because of his personal make-up, he is especially sensitive to this aspect of society today, which in its patriarchal/corporate phase has instilled fear of the spontaneous as a common emotional orientation. In being so sensitive, he feels for the rest of us. He brings our attention to this frustrated part of ourselves that we may have been over-looking. We identify with his sense of being held down and find satisfaction in further identifying with his characters in their noble quest. In skillfully depicting their drama, he taps into the archetype of rebellious freedom and escape from oppressiveness that makes the work irresistible, particularly to those who share a common inner orientation.

But let's look more closely at how he executes his work. We know from his biography that Kerouac did not possess the qualities he gave to his heroes. These were qualities he needed to retrieve or integrate from their repressed or undeveloped places. We know he did not enter into his art as a means to express what was bothering him, in order to get rid of it, to get it off his chest. If he had been following this "art therapy" approach to art, he would have directly shared his feelings of restriction in some way. Instead, he shares the opposite – what he *unconsciously* conceives to be the antidote.

In not directly portraying his inner conflict, it seems apparent he is not following a *product* approach to art making. The product would have been the known inner condition of restriction, but he is not particularly aware of the condition. Instead, he has come across a type of character that excites him by allowing a *positive process*, meaning process art that engages primarily positive feelings, to occur as he develops his art.

We can envision this happening as he plays around with stories and characters. It seems unlikely he intellectually chose these characters — they needed to develop and emerge over a period of time, allowing him to form an emotional attachment to them. He begins realizing that what really excites him are characters who take the archetype of rebellious freedom to the max, and he starts a novel. But still it is likely, in fact almost certain, that he is not aware of the inner restriction as the motive behind his attraction to this kind of character.

This unawareness is not to be seen as a flaw; as neither is the presence of the motive itself. These conditions are simply representative of the state of human evolution and the individual as a focal point of the collective. These are the factors that make life as we know it go around, and artists the trailblazers they are.

As with all artists working in process, he identifies strongly with the central characters as he works and re-shapes the writing. The identification is unconscious. This phase of art is euphoric and intoxicating. When we connect to our suppressed selves, *unconsciously* though the art, we feel whole and fulfilled. But at a certain point, identification becomes conscious and breaks down as we move into the next stage with the art; the bubble bursts. The creative, artistic euphoria takes a turn to cynicism, usually in exact proportion to the high that has swept us away, and the self-critical aspect of the art process hits.

This is the crucial point of any creative art endeavor that determines whether the art will be used for healing or not. If we do not successfully negotiate this final integrative phase, we do not move into healing. This is ultimately why artists do not heal with their work, why they turn to suppressive means to push down the darkness that appears, and how they can enter a vicious syndrome of creating, invoking the subconscious, and suppressing – what is called the manic-depressive cycle.

When the bubble bursts in this final stage, we see deeper. What we see is the motive – we see the darkness that is impelling us to long for, to create, and to identify with what we think will bring us into the light. But, as with any emotional process, darkness will not be eliminated by light alone. The darkness must be faced directly. It has been revealed through the art process; the process has served its purpose. If we turn from the darkness, we suppress it, and we fall into self-critical depression. Kerouac's life-long addiction to alcohol and the depressive condition in which Charters found him when she interviewed him towards the end of his life suggests he did not productively handle this stage of the art, but succumbed to the temptation to unwittingly suppress the negativity that was revealed.

To make the most of the art process, to use it as a means to personal evolution, we must take the darkness presented to us and work with it, both through conscious emotional processing and by recycling the darkness back into the art. To work with the darkness means to *integrate* it – to take it though the steps I have touched on. It means first, to become aware of it, and not turn away from it, thinking the art has let us down. It means accepting and experiencing the darkness as the means to balance it. It means recognizing that what we perceive as the critical voice is just the recognition of the darkness and has no rational reflection on the quality of the art.

All this may be aided by the inclusion of the darkness in the art as we create it. As process art continues, the artist introduces elements that mirror the pain that is uncovered within, in order to *be with* the pain and not avoid it. This is the essential element that gives art depth and makes it great as well as introduces the healing element. It allows the artist to transcend the collapse of the projection. The artist becomes *aware* of the feelings that have entered the art, and is no longer unconsciously enmeshed in them. As we look at Kerouac's work from this point of view, it is apparent that darkness has been included, even if it was not taken to the point of personal healing. Perhaps understated and implied, the pain and poignancy of his characters becomes evident as well as an enlightened, detached compassion for them.

To be fair with him, we should note that his artistic achievements represent an enormous goal realized. He did accomplish great work and made a significant contribution to contemporary culture. But in order to move his art experience to a healing level, Kerouac would have needed to see that the disproportionate, compulsive longing for wild, spontaneous freedom was a knee-jerk reaction to the subconscious inner feeling of being controlled and restricted, and that no amount of indulgence in the wildness, either in fantasy or reality, would bring about a resolution.

Next, he would need to *take responsibility*. It must be recognized that the experience of being controlled and restricted is the result of *inner blocking*, and is only *projected* upon the object that appears to be inflicting it. This is true even if there seems to be no question that some outside agency, such as father or society, is acting independently and cruelly upon him. Our psychic energies go out to mold and attract circumstances and obstacles in order to *bring our suppressed feelings into consciousness for clearing*. This is how karma operates and is the nature of our spiritual task.

Next, it is necessary to move to a place of *acceptance* regarding the inner feelings. It is very likely he would be in conflict with the authority figure – this is a natural reaction – but it would be a mistake to allow the resistance to carry over to his emotional experience. He must cease resistance to the feelings, accept them and move to a place where he can *experience* them. When he is finally able to experience, inwardly and fully, the control and restriction within himself, he becomes free of it. The art can be used to contain the feelings as he sits with them, watching them, experiencing them.

Some might argue that psychologically deconstructing Kerouac in this manner removes the magic and mystery from his art, and that if he had had an analyst to tell him these things, he never would have produced his books. But I disagree emphatically. I believe he, or any artist, would produce exactly the same art. We still need the art process to bring the shadow into the light. Becoming psychologically aware does not remove the impulse to create art; rather, the art process is made more rewarding. We are less apt to stumble around lost in the maze of subconscious forces we are attempting to bring forward and make sense of. We gain the opportunity to use the art for healing and personal evolution instead of being driven by it and ultimately sacrificing ourselves in bringing it to life. Indeed, as we enter deeply into the subjective mode necessary for the creation of art, we need all the guidance we can get.

## darkness in art

As we pursue process art, we follow what intuitively attracts us. We may not really understand why something draws us; we just know we are drawn to a certain object. The object represents, either as an abstract symbol or a concrete, representational image, parts of ourselves that have been exiled from our conscious sense of self; hence we feel incomplete. When we interact with or identify with the object, we experience a greater sense of wholeness and fulfillment, although we usually don't think in such terms.

The projected qualities can be either positive or negative, resulting in positive or negative process art; in both cases, we are attracted. In life, we are often compelled to possess people or objects when we project positive qualities onto them in the unconscious effort to regain these qualities for ourselves. Typical projected positive qualities include loveliness, softness, sweetness, strength, free-spiritedness, confidence, generosity, reliability, sensitivity, even happiness itself. However, the positive projection usually leads to disillusionment, because it is a false premise to begin with. Sooner or later, we are let down. Our hopes of wholeness are shattered, and we must regroup. Most of us who do not understand the unconscious process of projection simply try to find new objects on which to project: a new lover, friend, or job. We then proceed to experience the same cycle of projection and disappointment, not getting that we must find these qualities inside.

When we project negative qualities, such as selfishness, insignificance, weakness, ugliness, loneliness, forbidden sexual feelings and darkness in general, we often experience aversion and even hatred of the objects to which we attach our projection. The aversion we feel is a reflection of the rejection we carry within towards those qualities, and is not a function of the qualities themselves. Because we condemn our darkness, we condemn the object on which we project the darkness. Nonetheless, if we carefully look at our feelings, we will find that behind the aversion is an attraction for the same object. And the more powerful the aversion, the more powerful the attraction. We are attracted to the darkness in spite of ourselves, and often, this split in itself leads to great pain and confusion. The attraction to darkness exists because we need that repressed part of ourselves to make us whole.

As we move further down the road to enlightenment, we recognize that our aversion to many forms of darkness is just a conditioned mind-set. We outgrow the conditioning little by little, and as a result, our attraction to the darkness is no longer opposed. Even though, of course, we naturally exercise prudence about integrating dark elements into our lives, we recognize and are at peace with the realization that we are, indeed, attracted to darkness. We do not need to deny it. We understand that it is part of our evolutionary journey.

It's possible we might not allow ourselves to recognize an attraction to darkness. We might think we should always be associating with light, love, and happiness. Such positive feelings are of course important to our sense of well-being, and we would hope to be able to fill our lives with an abundant sense of them, and I do believe this is possible. Even though, from the holistic point of view, existence is composed of a balance of opposites, yin and yang, light and dark, I believe that life experience will be essentially positive when we begin to significantly uncover the suppressed subconscious and bring it into balance. We *transcend* the duality of light and dark. We reach a point where we are no longer affected in the same way by the so-called negative because our acceptance has freed us from it. We are unattached, and the negative is not experienced painfully. We are in balance. But in order to reach this point, we must engage the darkness.

As we allow darkness to enter our art creation, we begin the process of integration. Art provides a safe arena for these cut-off dark parts of ourselves. If we did not direct them into the art, they would no doubt appear projected in life, where they cause disruption and tempt us into acting them out. Sometimes artists believe they enhance their ability to feel life and make art by acting out darkness, but I believe this is always a mistake. A central purpose of art is to work out darkness in symbolic, safe ways, *in the art*. The experiencing of dark elements through the art is more effective in releasing their energies than any acting out in life might be.

Art that contains both light and dark images is the most fulfilling to produce and to experience, but in practice we often find that mature artists tend to lean in one direction or another, as their personal needs may suggest. Kerouac was drawn to the light, working with images of freedom and spontaneity, as compensation for the heaviness of restraint he most likely felt within. Another artist drawn towards the light in compensation for darkness was the quintessential Vincent van Gogh. His work has been described as an embodiment of mystical, transcendental, spiritual forces. But we know he was driven by intense darkness within, which he was never able to successfully integrate. Instead of using his art as a means to self-healing, it appears he allowed the cycle of projection and the subsequent uncovering of darkness within to overpower him.

In contrast, we see in the contemporary painter, Jean-Michel Basquiat, a predisposition to work directly with darkness, like many of today's most powerful artists, including visual artists, writers, film-makers, and musicians. This trend is now occurring in order to balance the global restriction that has allowed the collective shadow to build over long centuries of social, sexual, economic, and spiritual repression, by bringing the shadow into awareness for healing. The building of the collective shadow is what accounts for the incredible chaos we see in today's world. It seems all the suppression of past centuries is now coming up. That is why I view the current time as most challenging yet one which contains unprecedented opportunities for growth.

Basquiat's short life has been superbly portrayed in the film *Basquiat*, written and directed by Julian Schnabel, himself a successful artist. Basquiat's art and the manner in which he works, as represented in the film (actually paintings executed by Schnabel because the real work was not available) brilliantly typify the process approach to the subconscious. We see in his work the inner landscape brought directly into visual form. We see jagged edges, incongruities, sloppiness, ugliness, harshness and pain, but there is unmistakably a sense of *realness* permeating the work that makes it breathtaking. There is no question the work is magical. It represents the artist's handing over creation to the subconscious. It is not a product of the conscious ego, there is no sense of "look at me," even though, of course, Basquiat was driven by ego-needs as are we all. It is apparent that he was moved by, that he was attracted to, the portrayal of the negative shadow as a means to experience wholeness and peace, even though he may not have been able to articulate this motive. And because he was successful in its portrayal, the art reached the point of holding the archetypes of suffering, striving, freedom, and pathos with which we all can identify. It is tragic, however, that success as an artist does not automatically carry over to personal, emotional success; this is one of the points of the film. Basquiat died from a drug overdose at the age of 27.

In looking at the lives of van Gogh and Basquiat, we see artists who possessed enormous capacity for evocation of primal forces. Van Gogh uncovered the depths of darkness indirectly, to the same extent that he directly portrayed the spiritual; each of these forces must balance. Basquiat was impelled to directly uncover the negative in his art. Neither artist possessed the tools to use the art for ultimate self-healing or self-realization, and was unable to integrate the negativity that was uncovered. We might say that this is a peril of genius, if genius means the ability to see and feel deeply.

# 7

# The
# Three Stages
# Of Art

*Understanding and navigating the steps of art creation;*
*Working with feelings: Projecting, Recognizing,*
*Integrating; Emotional Processing*

The act of creating art consists of three stages. These stages, which apply to both product and process art, represent distinct orientations in how the artist experiences the art as it is being created. They are a natural sequence that occurs on a psychic-emotional level. Awareness of the three stages enables us to utilize artistic expression as a positive, fulfilling, growth experience. If we are not aware of the turns we may take, we may easily mismanage our experience, preventing the possibility of growth, or even hurting ourselves.

It is quite interesting to note that the stages include manic-depressive phases as a natural part of the cycle, which leads to trouble only when mishandled. The stages also account for the troublesome self-critical voice that results primarily from the unintegrated third stage.

## THE THREE STAGES OF ART

| STAGE | ACTIVITY | EXPERIENCE | CONDITION |
|-------|----------|------------|-----------|
| 1. Projecting | Inviting | Otherness | Fragmented |
| 2. Recognizing | Communing | Oneness | Manic |
| 3. Integrating | Revealing | Aloneness | Depressive |

In the first stage, we begin the art. We are in a normal state of consciousness. This condition is referred to as *fragmented* by psychologists, because it is the condition of suppression: we carry suppressed shadow parts of ourselves in our subconscious, cut off from our sense of conscious self. We are not whole; we are divided, fragmented, even though we are unaware of this. In the state of fragmentation, we unconsciously project those hidden parts of ourselves onto others, and we perceive them to be acting on us. Because we reject those parts of ourselves that we carry in the shadow – that's why they became part of the shadow in the first place – we reject them when they appear to our *unconscious* recognition, overlaid on others, as the result of our projection. We reject others, and perceive ourselves to be in an alienated, self-other universe. Our relationship to art is a microcosm of our relationship to life. Just as in life, we project parts of our hidden subconscious shadow into the art as we begin to create it, but the art at this stage has not yet come together; it seems difficult, unconnected, alien, fragmented. We relate to it as an *other*, as a prelude to reclaiming it.

In the second stage, we recognize our projection. As in stage one, our recognition is unconscious, but it's a different kind of unconsciousness. We still don't see that what we are looking at in the art represents a hidden part of ourselves, except possibly intellectually and theoretically. However, something happens in the way we perceive the projected part. We sense that we are in the presence of a part of ourselves from which we have been cut off. We become intensely attracted to the appearance of that part in the art, as a result of our innate longing for wholeness. We become enraptured and fascinated with the art. We identify with the art; we become it and it becomes us. We feel a colossal soul-communion in the reunion. We experience the oceanic blissfulness of *oneness*; otherness has ceased. The fact that the oneness takes place only on a certain level of our being does not limit the extent of our rapture. We allow the experience to engulf us, to take us over, so that it is all we see. In our oneness with the art object, we experience fulfillment. This experience is what has come to be called *manic*. We are euphoric; we can do no wrong; we are empowered, loving, finally happy. We do not see that our experience is part of a cycle, and that we will soon be entering the next stage.

In the inevitable third stage, the projection is revealed. We simply cannot maintain the oceanic condition indefinitely; the identification is broken, and we are shifted from oneness to *aloneness*. We become aware of the part of ourselves that has been in the background, impelling the tremendous high. Since that part is usually of a negative nature, we find ourselves with negative feelings that we cannot readily account for and, because we are focusing on the art, the art will generally appear to be causing the feelings. We will be fearful and anxious; or sad and jealous; or hurt and angry; or, most likely, our aloneness will turn to isolation. These are the kinds of feelings that will emerge from the subconscious shadow as preliminary manifestations of deeper patterns that will need to be brought into the light.

The movement into the third stage is inherently depressive. In the previous high, huge amounts of psychic energy were used to maintain the condition. We are bound to feel let down and in the need of recharging when we leave it. This is *authentic depression* that must be accepted and nurtured. When we add the awareness of the negativity that has just emerged into consciousness to this inherent depressiveness, we are faced with a condition that must be approached with extreme care if it is not to overpower us.

But often we are overpowered. We do not expect the sudden change; we are disillusioned; we are at a loss to explain or handle our feelings. Essentially, we have gone through the exact same stages as a love affair, except that instead of another person, we have used the inanimate art object as our projection screen. The fall from the high of the second stage triggers the self-critical voice. In our disillusionment, and with the emergence of the negative, we find fault with the art, just as we do with the lover, thinking that the cause of our pain is in the other. We do not see that the cause of the pain is within.

We will examine these three stages in detail, establishing a strategy that will enable us to successfully navigate the art path that presents such difficult challenges yet contains equivalent potentials for inner fulfillment.

# First Stage: Projecting

To invite art means to set the stage for the appearance of the subconscious. The subconscious resides on a different plane of being, with different rules, from that with which we are ordinarily familiar. There is a sense of timelessness when we shift to this plane of consciousness; everything is happening at once. We can quickly manifest what we want simply by visualizing it, and thinking of another place transports us there immediately. This realm of consciousness has been called the astral plane or the fourth dimension, and we will naturally have trouble comprehending it with our three-dimensional, dualistic minds. We have referred to it as the magical realm, where feelings predominate.

The astral plane has been described as much larger in scope than the earth plane, with an aliveness that earth experience cannot match. It is said to be the next plane of human beingness after we leave this earth life behind. As represented in occult literature, the astral plane is the emotional plane. It is the place where suppressed feelings are held, and we experience the results of that suppression directly when we reach into the consciousness of the astral, which we may do in several ways.

Dreams are a primary way to contact the astral. Dreaming is a category of consciousness that covers a wide spectrum of activity. Ancient cultures and esoteric lore propose that we routinely leave our physical bodies in sleep to journey in the astral body. Our level of consciousness determines the type of astral dream we encounter and what we will remember upon awakening. Our experience may be entirely mundane and based on physical perceptions during sleep, for example, or may range to what is called lucid dreaming, where we "wake-up" in the dream state. Then, deep aspects of the personal and collective subconscious are revealed and experienced through image, sound, and touch as metaphoric drama with a sense of realness, presence, and power that exceeds normal earth consciousness. The key factor in working with dreams is to under-stand that although the subconscious is revealed in the dream state, as in the art state, we must deliberately work with the material in our ordinary consciousness to release it. There is little inherent clearing that occurs simply by having the dream and its accompa-nying feelings; otherwise, all humanity would be liberated.

In death, we leave the earthly body behind, and transition into the astral, where we encounter fully all levels of our suppressed selves. We know this unconsciously and intuitively, and we often dread the meeting; it may not really be death that we fear but the confrontation with ourselves. In religious terms, we come face to face with our personal heaven and hell – the feelings we have allowed to remain buried in the subconscious. Understanding this, we may be encouraged to explore and release the subconscious now, when we can do so with control and effectiveness. In fact, it is recognized by esoteric tradition that being on the earth represents a tremendous *opportunity* for releasing feelings – the same as clearing karma – which is not available to the same degree on the astral, even though our awareness is greatly increased.

As the next higher plane of consciousness, the astral, or emotional, plane represents the field in which we need to work as we advance on the path of personal and collective evolution. We can see the need for this all around us. The emotions are poorly understood. We are all in emotional turmoil. There is no teaching of this critical topic in our schools, because there is no tradition of knowledge in Western society from which our teachers may draw. All education is intellectual, or left-brained. And even our therapists are not sure how to deal with this area; there is disagreement about what constitutes effective emotional work. As artists, we seek to work with feelings, but often do not have the basic knowledge of the principles of feeling work.

## entering the flow

The astral plane is the place where art comes from. In order to intentionally contact this hidden emotional realm, consciousness must be altered so it resonates with astral frequencies. Most artists do this intuitively. We immerse ourselves in art; we live, breathe, eat art. We get ourselves in tune, to the point where the subconscious is stirred and encouraged to come forward. We employ non-destructive means to enter this mode of being: relaxation of body and mind through meditation, yoga, breathwork, movement, and ritual all move us into a feeling orientation. We enter what can be called *trance*, a non-ordinary state of being centered in the right-brain. We understand that entering the altered state with the aid of drugs may appear efficacious, and that they may even be used occasionally and judiciously, with a sense of reverence as did Native Americans, but that they can be addictive and destructive. Indeed, as we engage in consciousness work and the proper use of art, it is likely we will no longer feel the need for stimulants.

In our preliminary experience in trance, we may sit blankly, or stare at the ocean, clouds, or grass; or watch the breath, a candle, or a sensation in the body; or listen to the silence, or to the traffic. We may engage any randomly formed stimulus. We cultivate the sense of detachment, of both externals and whatever inner feelings may be evoked by them. We *witness*. Developing the witness capacity corresponds to development of the soul. It may not come overnight, but it grows stronger as we dedicate ourselves to growth and to our art.

As artists, to help enter the creative flow we can move to our NOW practice – non-directed, non-edited, stream of consciousness engagement in our media. We scribble or splash paint; we make random sounds and chords; we write nonsense. We open. We release production of image, sound, or word from conscious control. We allow ourselves *to be led*, guided by what attracts us. We allow spontaneous happenings to enter the art, even and maybe especially in the form of accidents.

Right from the beginning, we emphasize that the most important aspect of the work is not *what* we are manifesting, but *who* is doing the manifesting. Is it our conscious ego, or are we stepping aside, inviting the subconscious to appear as we surrender control to some other – we may not know what – guiding intelligence? Do we grant the process a life of its own? This focus on relinquishing control, right from the beginning, is the most important element in entering the creative art flow. The famous classical artist Raphael advises to "think of something else" when making art, in order to get the conscious, controlling, limited mind out of the way. It may not be necessary to think of something else – just stilling the mind, or in the third stage to be with the feelings that are evoked, is enough to get the conscious mind out of the way and to make ready for guidance. When guidance occurs, we feel its presence and importance. Something authentic seems to have happened. We are awed and we trust.

If we retain a strong ego involvement with the work, it will not be as easy for guidance to come in. If we are too proud of our technique, too attached to the final result to let go, if the acceptance of the work means we are accepted, if we must achieve a certain result to satisfy ourselves or the client, we produce work in which the subconscious may not appear. Thus, professionalism may work against us. We gain expertise in execution and esthetics, but the work may not be soulful. Work becomes soulful when the subconscious is allowed to enter.

## evoking

Sometimes, we may wish to enter the art flow from a specific starting point. We may have a particular personal condition, feeling, or question we wish to explore through the art, to clarify or clear. We begin by making an intention. We then make a representative image of the condition, feeling, or question *as it appears to us now,* in whatever media we choose. It is important to note that we do not try to portray the answer, we only portray the condition about which we are seeking guidance. But then we must be careful to go beyond the directed nature of product mode. We have to shift to process, drop the ego's control of the image, and let the subconscious speak through the evolving image.

As we gain facility in evoking the subconscious, we find that images spontaneously appear that demand to be made manifest. We will recognize these images from the urgency that accompanies them; it will feel as if they are jumping into form. They can appear anytime, but will probably come forward most frequently when the conscious mind is disengaged, such as when we are doodling with materials or instruments, or during meditation or sleep, when the images appear as dreams. This image-making tendency of the subconscious, whether appearing to our inner sight as visual image, sound, movement, or word, is in itself quite interesting and representative of the mind's innate tendency to portray subconscious contents in metaphoric form, as an "other."

As the images appear, it is likely we will not see their relevance at first. We may be uncomfortable with them, or even dislike them, yet we recognize that they must represent something of importance for us. Because we are still in the fragmented stage, these emerging elements seem alien. The art, although it is proceeding, has not yet "come together." "Accidents" that happen in the production are seen as unwanted and not as the introduction of completely new ways of perceiving with which we are gifted.

## struggle

The first stage is often associated with struggle. The coming together takes longer than expected; we become frustrated; we are unsatisfied, unmoved, unable to bring the art to life; we can't make all the pieces work. Life circumstances themselves become formidable obstacles to producing art; sometimes just finding time for the art, not to mention the often demoralizing struggle to market the art once it is completed, can be major problems.

We usually don't see that it is we who unconsciously create the struggle. If we were patient, unattached, non-compulsive, non-addicted, non-abusive, and non-dependent on our art, we would not experience any struggle. We would be happy with wherever the art was. We would have no agenda and no disappointment, but possibly we would have no reason to create the art in the first place. The reality is that we *are* often impatient with the process, attached to results, compulsive about execution, addicted to the highs, abusive of chemicals and the sanctity of the art, and dependent upon getting our ego needs met.

We experience pain for all these reasons. This pain, being reflected by our surroundings, circumstances, or relationships, is somewhat different from the pain we meet when we glimpse the subconscious through art. We may therefore tend to minimize it, invalidate it, or try to get rid of it so we can get on with the art. But we must recognize that the pain of the struggle is another kind of projection, and that we must honor it and process it as an integral part of our personal growth just as we process the pain that emerges more directly through the art. The art arena becomes the place where we work out all these inner levels.

As we become familiar with the experience of other artists, both famous and not, and with our own overall experience in producing finished art, it seems apparent that much art is accompanied by struggle, and that great art is often accompanied by great struggle. Whether this is a requirement of great art is a question that each of us will need to answer individually.

Philosophically speaking, the suggestion arises that, on the energetic level, the pain of the struggle that goes into the art is what gives it the vitality that makes it great. But, even if this is true – and I am not implying that it need be although I must admit that all of my own productions in both writing and music have always been accompanied by tremendous struggle – it does not mean we must create struggle in order to have something to put into the art. Many artists, both novice and veteran, fall into the trap of consciously or unconsciously creating struggle in their lives and relationships, thinking they will be able to put more soul into the work. Such "soulfulness" is inauthentic and superficial. We don't need to go out of our way to create struggle; if we need to encounter it, it will be there.

## Second Stage: Recognizing

In this stage, we enter into the state of rapture with the art that is emerging under our hand. Just as with a new lover, we feel that incredible wholeness that comes from meeting those parts of ourselves previously hidden. We want to merge with the art; we can't stand to be away from it; we are completely attracted and fascinated. Although we may theoretically understand that the art represents an aspect of ourselves with which we are being reunited, it is unlikely we will at first completely recognize that aspect. Our recognition is *subliminal* – below the threshold of consciousness – but nevertheless, we know we are in the midst of a powerful experience of oneness.

In the second stage, the function of the art is to *hold* the feelings. It can also be said that the art holds the projection. One of the motives for projection in general is that it is less threatening, easier, and safer to find feelings outside of ourselves instead of looking directly to the inner. The feelings are held, or *contained*, in the art, and the artist interacts with the art as a means to eventual self-realization.

As discussed, the artistic content may be either positive or negative, or a mixture. Both types are necessary for wholeness. We may see the heights of idealism or the lows of despair in the art, but our experience is enraptured regardless of the type of content. The rapture comes over us because of the wholeness that we experience, not because the content is intrinsically joyous. In this way, the artist connects to a transcendental, unconditional, spiritual dimension.


## emergence

When engaging art, it is helpful to keep in mind that the eventual goal is to become fully conscious of and to *integrate* the aspect that is finding form in the art; to use the art as an emotional and spiritual journey to wholeness. To integrate means to reclaim, to rejoin with that split-off, feeling-based, repressed part of ourselves, to become whole. Previously the aspect was rejected and banished to the subconscious; now, it is in a precarious state, emerging into consciousness, but not yet completely there.

In order to facilitate integration, there are two ways we might proceed. The first is the way of science, the way of the intellect. We might try to question and understand what is appearing in the art that is so emotionally meaningful. This approach was first used in the early days of art therapy, when analysis was in vogue. Art was seen as a product of the subconscious, which was thought to be knowable through intellectual effort. However, I believe that using analysis as the main route to integration is self-defeating. It removes us from the magical feeling realm – the realm where integration takes place. It keeps us in the left-brain, unaware of any higher form of perception.

The other way to effect integration is to stay with the feelings. The art has emerged spontaneously as a gift from the subconscious. It has become alive because we are projecting into it. Rather than question it, probe it, tear at it, we allow it to retain its mystery. We do not seek with the intrusive, intellectual left-brain that must know "what it means." We remain in the intuitive right-brain. We allow the feeling experience, the mystery, to build. We linger with the feelings contained and reflected in the images that emerge in the art. We reverently engage the art, communing with it, letting it work on us more and more deeply, letting new feelings come forward that were initially hidden as the work progresses, allowing ourselves to come more and more into contact with our forgotten selves.

The art becomes a means for us *to be with* the feelings. As we are taken from feeling to feeling, from level to level, the feelings change from bright to dark and back again. All through the journey, we are spellbound by their emergence. We may not know what the work is finally saying to us – what aspects of the suppressed subconscious are coming forth – until weeks, months, or years after we feel finished with it. This is characteristic of authentic work that genuinely evokes the subconscious and is not merely illustrating a known or pre-conceived image.

At a certain point, the personal issues we explore in the art will bring us into contact with the archetypes of feeling, especially if we have been allowing ourselves to be led by the work. We reach to universal joy as well as pain. We see that our loneliness, our frustration, our sense of insignificance is common to all. We are empowered by this realization. We can more easily accept our emotional experience. We can more easily step back, view it dispassionately, allow it *to be* with a sense of peace and inner poise, and allow ourselves to be replenished by the power of the archetypes, both positive and negative, as we touch them. Contacting universal experience through the archetypes, by starting with the personal, brings great fulfillment in the practice of art.

# engulfment

The powerful experiences of coming into wholeness and engaging the archetypes can be the basis for another difficulty to which we are susceptible in the second stage of art: we may be swept away. We allow the inherently *manic* identification with the emerging self to overwhelm us, to dominate us. We lose the sense of separation of emotion and self. We are lost in the identification. We become addicted to it, compulsive about maintaining it, caught up in it, engulfed. The loss of perspective and ourselves in the art results in ungrounding. We set ourselves up for the manic-depressive cycle. *Engulfment* must be guarded against. It is another snare of art-consciousness work that can be avoided by being aware of and maintaining the boundary and balance between self and art.

The predisposition to engulfment is found in personality types that are addictive. An addictive personality is always looking for something to attach to, something outside itself that will sustain it, take it out of its isolation, give it meaning. It seeks to establish dependency instead of developing inner resources. Recognizing this impulse in oneself and not yielding to it is the first step to working with engulfment. It is good for the art to give us sustenance and joy – why else would we do it – but, as in relationships, we must be careful.

To loosen the hold of engulfment, we must become *grounded*. Ungrounded, we are susceptible. Grounding may be thought of in literal terms. Start by establishing a psychic connection to the earth. Visualize yourself standing with feet on the earth, perhaps arms raised overhead to bring in the energy of the sun. Allow the connection to the earth to sustain you. Allow negativity to be drawn to the earth. Feel the primal feminine essence of the earth energy. Feel the feelings in your body. Feel yourself as a powerful independent being. Include moderate exercise in your lifestyle. Eat properly. Use yoga and breathwork. *Witness.*

Engulfment is compounded by contact with what is referred to as the *elemental* forces of the archetypes. These natural forces are raw and primal and alluring. They can manifest as both positive or negative. We can be drawn to them like a moth to a flame. Controlled contact with them can be beneficial, but too much can be harmful. In a way, we are playing with fire when we open to the subconscious through art. Even though I believe we are essentially guided and protected by the higher intelligence to which we surrender in our process, sometimes we go out of our way to act contrary to what we know are our best interests. The elemental force of rage, for instance, which exists as part of the collective subconscious as a pure essence, can take us over if we invite it. We may be controlled by it, driven by it, experience it out of proportion to any personal suppressed content.

When we are taken over by an elemental force, a force not originating in our personal suppressed subconscious, we have reached the stage that is termed *psychotic* by the medical establishment. This stage is another dangerous characteristic associated with the artistic temperament, but is sometimes viewed with awe and even romanticism because of the immense power and lack of inhibition psychotics can display as a result of contact with primal forces.

However, these deeply distraught persons are lost to their personal evolutionary path and use the power at their disposal in an attempt to compensate for their distress, engendering a particularly intense form of the manic-depressive syndrome. They are being used, impersonally, by destructive cosmic forces, and must sever the connection to the wildness before they can come into themselves.

Psychosis is usually accompanied by a highly damaged aura that has lost its psychic protective function, which is typically brought about through drug, alcohol, smoking, or sexual abuse, and to a lesser extent by nutritional deficiencies, workaholism, stress, chronic emotional self-rejection, and exposure to environmental pollution. Reversal of these conditions would be the first steps to healing. Most of us will not experience these extreme dangers with art. Some moderate degree of loss of self in the identification with the art will be unavoidable, but should not pose any obstacle to the overall art process.

At a certain point, we find that the idyllic second stage of the art process comes to an end. Projection cannot be maintained indefinitely; it is not nature's intention. When projection ends, we enter the unavoidable third stage of art. The manner in which we handle this stage determines whether our evolution will move forward or will regress, and whether art will be healing or not.

## Third Stage: Integrating

In the third stage of art, projection ceases as it becomes conscious. We become aware of what has been in the wings, enticing us with visions of wholeness. Even though we may have been working with images of pain, they have been images that the art has possessed, not us. We have enjoyed a kind of fairy-tale relationship to them. They have been accompanied by the ecstasy of the creative act. We have not really seen that they are indeed within us. Now, we see. It is revealed to us that the pain is inside, again through feeling. Just as with a lover, the art has served its purpose, evoking from us that which we were not ready to receive, preparing us, even strengthening us, for the ultimate confrontation with ourselves.

## the ending of projection

When projection ends, we are let down. The art, which has been the center of our world, no longer supports us. Our buoyant effervescence changes to somber colorlessness; our blissful sense of oneness to aloneness. The critical voice speaks; depression sets in; the painful feelings that have been revealed are amplified by anxiety. All this is unavoidable. It is inherently part of the third stage, the result of projection, and must be accepted and handled correctly.

But usually we prefer to run, employing whatever frantic means we have cultivated to avoid experience and suppress it. That's what happens if we don't handle this stage correctly. We re-suppress the feelings that have been occupying us for all this time with the art process. We defeat the purpose of the creative art process, and hinder our emotional and spiritual healing.

The depression of the third stage of art is an authentic part of the art cycle that must be accepted. By expecting that a low will follow the high, by not demanding that we be on top all the time, by taking time to rest and recover, we allow a recharging that will bring us again to the peak of the cycle. Just this simple stance can be instrumental in reversing depression.

The inherent depressiveness of the third stage is amplified when we do not successfully move to integration with the emerging aspect of ourselves. The habitual response of aversion, avoidance, and re-suppression of emerging feelings creates a mood of despondency. We expend considerable psychic energy in suppressing the feelings, leading to a deeper level of energetic depletion, the primary cause of what we call depression. We then often seek to relieve the depression through means that develop into addictions. As we repeatedly engage in this cycle, we allow a large body of suppressed feelings to accumulate and we move deeper into the manic-depressive syndrome.

Integration means making the aspect of ourselves that was split-off and projected into the art part of ourselves again. We accomplish this primarily by acceptance and experience of the associated feelings. There is no question that integration is challenging, but there is also no question that it is much better to engage than to avoid, either out of ignorance or choice. In avoidance, we continue the build-up of feelings that undermines the possibility of optimal life experience. We keep setting ourselves up for failure and we stay depressed.

When you see clearly that it is much more beneficial and even easier to work with feelings than to avoid them, and to align yourself with the evolutionary, growth-oriented life principle, you gain the will and fortitude to enter the work with resolve. And once you have done so, you find that the work is not so daunting after all. The higher self *is* guiding you; you *are* given just what you can handle. Most of all, you experience true fulfillment from engaging and clearing feelings, allowing authentic emotional and spiritual growth to occur. This growth is a central purpose of life on the earth plane.

The kinds of feelings that are engaged in the third stage will range from what we call first-level feelings to core feelings. First-level feelings are usually more emotional; they tend to come up first in the uncovering process. For example, you may experience anger, fear, anxiety, sexual frustration and compulsiveness, heartbreak, jealousy, or any emotion. As you process any of these, you come upon deeper core feelings. Behind the emotion of anger may be the feeling of rejection, invalidation, futility, or failure. Behind the emotion of fear may be the feeling of insecurity. Behind the emotion of sexual frustration and compulsiveness may be the feeling of basic emotional-psychic neediness and hunger. Behind the heartbreak and jealousy may be the feeling of self-hatred, and so on. These feelings are only examples of what may linger behind the emotions. They are not the only correlations; you must uncover your own core feelings. In entering the process through your art, you will be continually led to personal, deeper levels of the hidden self important to you that need the light of consciousness.

In the third stage, you may not need to use the art as a focus for integration work, although this is possible. You may choose to put aside the art for the time being and work directly with the painful feelings that have been actualized into consciousness. The art has served as a powerful tool, bringing up the feelings, and they become the focus of awareness.

In fact, in my own personal work, this is my preference. I find that the feeling that has emerged is so central in my consciousness I no longer need the art to reveal it or contain it. I engage the feeling in my sitting practice. In a way, for the time being, I feel I have transcended the need for the art. The art seems flat anyway, as if it would require effort to go back to it; my soul is no longer in it. But this still represents being in the third stage of the art. The feelings that the art have revealed must now be integrated, not only for the completion of the art-healing process, but to get back to a place where I will more objectively be able to see the art.

In this third stage, before the integration takes place, our vision of the art is highly skewed. It seems unsatisfactory; the critical voice has set in. In practice, we may oscillate between all stages during the art process. We may come into stage three, sit with our feelings, experience the shifting that signifies integration, and go back to stage one or two as we continue with the development of the piece, allowing a deeper level to emerge.

## emotional processing

If you choose to continue to use the art to contain the feelings you are processing, you would keep sitting with the art, allowing it to serve as a *stimulus* for the feelings, just as you would use a memory of a past experience in a therapy session. You might close your eyes from time to time, holding the image in your inner vision. You have shifted from a primarily mental mode to a feeling mode. You are in the witness, silently watching your feelings as they now are reflected by the art.

Your focus is different from stage two. Now, you are highly conscious that you are looking into a mirror. You are seeing yourself naked for the first time, in contrast to stage two, where everything had a rosy glow and seemed perfect. You are more somber, more humble in the presence of your truth, but you are also wise, because you understand what is happening, and this knowledge gives you the power to be able to manage your experience.

To work with feelings the art has revealed, you *process* them, either with or without the art. You look into the heartbreak, the loneliness, the fear, and perhaps the patterns of behavior that you have established in response to them. If you engage the feelings with awareness, taking responsibility, consciously accepting, being with them, experiencing them deeply, witnessing them – you will move into healing.

At this point, although the art has helped in accessing the subconscious, working with feelings that have emerged through the art is the same as working with feelings that come up in everyday life or in meditation. We have been touching upon how to work with these feelings throughout this book, but for an in-depth discussion of this vital topic, I must again refer you to *Emotional Clearing*. However, to further get you moving in the right direction, I will summarize the steps here. These steps may be applied to any feeling, including depression, that has been revealed through your art. The four steps, or conditions, are:

*Awareness*
*Acceptance*
*Direct Experience*
*Transformation*

Sit quietly, and approach your feelings from each of these four viewpoints in succession, but note that all four conditions must be present simultaneously for successful integration.

## awareness

Take responsibility for your feelings. In so doing, you empower yourself for healing. You have unknowingly created your present experience through mismanagement of feelings. If you have created your experience, you can also undo it. You have suppressed certain feelings in the past, creating a debt that must be paid, by simply accepting and experiencing the feelings that are now calling for attention. You are not alone in this condition, it is common to us all, and comprises the work we are to do in this present stage of consciousness evolution. It is our *karma*.

The feelings have become known to you through projection upon your art or others. Use projection to your advantage. Do not fight it but rather see through it. Understand that you are projecting, own your feelings, and work with them. Strive to become aware of the real feelings that emerge through the art. They may be actively emotional, such as anger, fear, loneliness, or hatred; or they may be more subdued, such as rejection, failure, insignificance, or resentment. They may be first-level or core feelings. As you stay with any feeling, you will be led to deeper levels of your healing process.

## acceptance

Resistance to a feeling is what caused it to become suppressed initially and what keeps it suppressed. Move to a place of acceptance of the feeling. Look deeply within, to the unconscious, conditioned resistance that makes you turn away from this aspect of yourself. Do you indulge in avoidance behavior – behavior calculated to take you out of the feeling – including acting out, controlling, analyzing, substance or relationship addiction, activity, and especially blame? With regard to art, undue preoccupation with interpretation, with finding the meaning, can also serve as a self-rejecting mechanism, keeping us in the head instead of the feeling centers of the body.

Modify these patterns of behavior as best as possible, allowing the feeling to come more fully into view, no longer obscured. As the feeling is progressively released, you will experience a natural and easy withdrawal from these destructive avoidance behaviors, since they will be no longer required.

Extend to the feeling a sense of being heard, validated, cared for, accepted, in contrast to the rejection it previously experienced. The shift from self-rejection to self-acceptance, on the feeling level, is experienced profoundly. You enter a new relationship with yourself, which leads to healing, balance, and authentic self-love.

## direct experience

As the feeling comes into view, it must be experienced to clear. If you are new to holistic healing work, you may not be comfortable with the idea of opening to your feelings. I hope it will suffice here to know that proper experiencing of a feeling is not the same as wallowing in it or being overcome by it. Nor does opening to a feeling mean you are giving it permission or encouraging it to continue or grow. On the contrary, deliberately experiencing the feeling is what it needs to be satisfied, and to dispel.

Allow yourself to *be with* the feeling, to watch it impassively and choicelessly. Feel it on a body level, shifting out of the mental level. As you practice doing this, you will gain a familiarity with this shifting – the mind becomes still, and the stillness allows you to see through to the feeling previously obscured by the mental activity. Engage the feeling fully. Experience it as an energetic condition, vibrating completely through your body without resistance. As you open yourself to direct feeling, you open the door to the healing energies of the universe. Allow them to come in, and feel the replenishment.

Bodywork, in the form of yoga, movement, energetic polarity, therapeutic massage or any form that appeals to you can be helpful in breaking up energetic blocks that are usually present. Yoga breathwork is also effective. Develop a regular practice of sitting with feelings, being with them, giving them the voice into your consciousness that they require for healing. Trust that you are being guided; that you will be given only what you can handle.

## transformation

*Witnessing* introduces the key spiritual element into the healing process. Witnessing is essential. Without it, we are immersed and identified with the feeling, and healing will not occur. Witnessing means to step back, to become impassive, to watch the feeling instead of being drawn into it, to break the identification. The breaking of the identification with the feeling has already happened to a certain extent with the third stage of the art; you must not resist it, but allow it to develop. You will arrive at a new kind of consciousness that is able to look at what is going on, and be part of it, but also be detached.

Witnessing is a movement to the higher-self. As you dwell in the higher-self witness, you watch the lower-self body, mind, and feelings, where the turmoil is taking place. The witness place is always calm, timeless, in the moment, without choice. Choice is not an issue because the witness is at ease with whatever is happening in the lower self. It accepts fully *what is*. Witnessing allows the full participation of the healing energies of the universe. They come in spontaneously, finding the places that need to be healed. As you release held feelings, you move to a place of transcendence.

Lack of integration in the third stage results in devaluing the whole art process with which we have been absorbed. In the back of our minds, we know we have not completed something that is calling us, but we may not know what that something is. When we are aware of the nature of the art process – that we are being drawn to a lost part of ourselves – we gain the will to proceed to integration.

Reclaiming aspects of ourselves is preceded by the awareness and integration of corresponding but often contrary feelings. For example, to reclaim assertiveness means to integrate feelings of shyness and lack of worth; to reclaim freedom means to integrate feelings of being limited and oppressed; to regain strength means to integrate feelings of weakness; to regain love is to integrate hate, and so on. All these negative feelings must be honored, accepted, felt, and allowed to tell their story of how they were invalidated, pushed down, not heard. Then, we move to a place of balance, where both dualistic aspects, positive and negative, co-exist in a basically harmonious experience. Neither is suppressed, and we accept each within ourselves. We recognize that neither could exist without the other. We trust in our feelings, knowing they are always right for us.

Transcendence occurs when opposites come into balance. In balance, we no longer feel compulsively driven to possess the positive in a frantic attempt to avoid the negative. We transcend; we go beyond being caught up in any particular dualistic manifestation of consciousness. We are no longer stuck.

The actual experience of transcendence need not be mysterious and unattainable, as the word might suggest. Transcendence happens with regard to everyday, mundane concerns. For example, we process our disappointment, taking responsibility for it, feeling it, and soon we note a shifting of our inner experience. We are no longer disappointed. We have gone beyond the issue in question. We have grown. Through such repeated successes, we find ourselves at a much different point in our lives after only a short period, say six months or a year, than if we continued with our customary unenlightened ways of reacting to feelings. And, perhaps most importantly, with each success we experience a genuine sensation of joy, the result of positive growth. We know we are moving in the right direction.

# part 3

Feelings About Making Art

# 8

# Fine-Tuning

*Avoiding stumbling on the art path; The critical voice;*
*Artist's block; Burn-out; Support; Recognition;*

## the critical voice

The third stage of art gives rise to the critical voice. When the projection of the previous stage is made conscious, we fully see the darkness that has been behind it. The elation we have been experiencing in the passionate reunion with the lost part of ourselves, even a negative feeling or quality, is replaced by a somber awareness. We come face to face with our harsh, naked selves. Often, we resent the abrupt shift, and we hold the art responsible. Unthinkingly, we *defend* from the realization of the inner feelings.

To defend means to adopt an inner posture that is assumed will keep feelings away. A painful feeling comes up, and we defend from it by any number of means. The simplest is that we shut down. We close ourselves off from the feeling and the object we perceive to be causing the feeling. We can escape into drugs, activity, sex, TV, anything, as a means to defend from the feeling, which, of course, results in its suppression.

A popular strategy used to defend from painful feelings is blame. When we blame some other person, circumstance, or object for a painful feeling, we succeed in defending against the feeling. The feeling becomes blocked and is not accessible to the true, deep, inner experiencing it needs in order to be released. It is even possible to blame ourselves, which is called guilt, and achieve the same blocking.

The critical voice is a blameful voice. We think the art is causing the painful feelings we have come upon in the third stage, and we blame the art in the effort to defend. The blame extends easily into blanket condemnation, and we find endless fault, doubting the quality of the work and so on. The trap is exactly the same that is experienced with a lover. When projection upon the lover ends, we come face-to-face with the pain inside. Instead of taking responsibility, we blame our lover in the attempt to avoid the pain.

Another way of looking at how the critical voice forms is to see it as an extension of the *rejection* we tend to apply to feelings revealed in the third stage of the art. Rather than honoring them and moving to a place of acceptance, we reject them because they make us uncomfortable. But rejection is what caused the feelings to be suppressed in the first place. In order to move into integration and healing, the rejection must be reversed with genuine *acceptance*, which eventually results in deep self-acceptance and self-love. Often, however, the rejection carries over to the art. We think the art is responsible for the feelings coming up; it is making us fearful or lonely or anxious. We condemn the art for doing this and begin the vicious cycle of the critical voice.

To handle the critical voice means first, to understand how it comes about: as a result of trying to avoid feelings that have been revealed. Then, we must place the critical voice aside and start to work with the primary feelings that have emerged through the art. Correctly handling the third stage, and not turning away from the feelings revealed, is central to restraining the critical voice.

We may hear the critical voice, but we know it does not necessarily represent any objective, correct evaluation of the art; it is inherently irrational. It is us *defending, blaming, rejecting ourselves* through the art, in an attempt to avoid feelings. We must stay detached from the voice, letting it behave in its irrational, childlike way, possibly treating it as a child who must be seen and heard in order to experience the acceptance it needs, but who is not allowed to seriously influence the adult.

If we can maintain this stance, we may find that the critical voice actually has some significant input. But we only see this if we maintain detachment. If we resist the critical voice and try to make it go away, we are likely to suppress it, as with any other part of ourselves that we condemn. When suppressed, the critical voice will be projected upon others. We will feel criticized and unsupported by them even when they are genuinely encouraging. If we strongly reject the critical voice, we attract people to us who will actually criticize us harshly, mirroring that part of ourselves from which we have turned away.

## artist's block

In the film *Wonder Boys*, Michael Douglas plays a writer who "doesn't believe in writer's block." The novel he's been working on, for more than a few years, is now up to 2600 pages. What the character doesn't realize is that he is paralyzed by fear that this book, his second, will not be the huge success the first one was, and he cannot finish it and put it out there. His blocking is not in terms of output, but in terms of completion, and he is probably escaping into the art to avoid his feelings of fear.

Yet, in many ways, I also don't believe in artist's block. I believe it's always possible to sit down and allow art to happen, whatever form it takes for you. You can always sketch, write a paragraph, work in the clay, and find comfort there, watching as the artistic creative process unfolds under your hands.

What we often mean when we say we are blocked is that our work does not meet certain requirements we have for it. We judge it, and find it lacking. We feel blocked that we cannot produce "good" work. However, we have discussed that art is under the control of the subconscious mind. We are merely observers. The sooner we relinquish conscious control of the art and drop all expectations about what it should be and what it should look like, the sooner we will get past the feeling of being "blocked." We allow the work to take on its own life, and evolve on its own schedule and with its own characteristics. This is how meaningful art is produced, art that is new to us, art that reveals, and is not just a reflection of our conscious ego.

Sometimes, however, we do find ourselves unable to access the inspirational voice within that needs to enter the art for it to be significant and fulfilling to ourselves and others. We find that approaching our art brings up anxiety, making it impossible to relax into the process. The self-critical voice paralyzes us. We are unable to complete work, re-doing it over and over. During such periods, it may be said that we are encountering artist's block.

We all experience periods of being blocked from artistic work; they are part of the regular cycle of creativity. Accepting these dry spells, seeing them as periods of replenishing, and riding them out will often be all that is needed. Only when blocking is chronic does it suggest a more serious condition. To demystify chronic blocking, and to understand how we ourselves create it, we must turn to an examination of our relationship with our feelings.

As we have discussed, we often unconsciously fall into the trap of suppressing feelings instead of allowing them to complete their cycles in our awareness. In essence, we create a block to the feelings, keeping them in the subconscious. It is this same block that inhibits the creative flow.

*Blocking of feelings results in artist's block.*

We eagerly respond to the artistic impulse, but we forget about the other side of ourselves that actively keeps pushing the feelings away. We become split, cut off from the subconscious, the source of our creativity. The anxiety we experience results from the intense approach/avoidance conflict that arises when we try to access deeper levels within.

The blocking of the inner self is perhaps most evident in work in which we try to explore some aspect of darkness. If we are blocking these feelings within, dark aspects will not find their way into the work. Dark images that do appear will not be deeply felt, or will have an inauthentic or "made-up" sense about them. The work lacks the sense of *truth* that real art needs; it seems insipid, lifeless, phony, hypocritical. The blocking we create to shield ourselves from the negative subconscious also carries over to the higher, positive energies, limiting our access to them. We inadvertently block ourselves from the realization of love and happiness.

Blocking may be thought of as extreme suppression, or repression, where we have no awareness at all of the feelings that are rejected. The normal condition for most of us at this stage of our personal evolution is one of suppression. There is no reason to be alarmed at this. If we recognize suppression and how it contributes to the projections we experience, either in life or art, and make conscious, informed efforts towards integration of the projections – as we do in the three stages of art – we fall in step with evolution and fulfillment. In blocking, however, we are even unable to move to a place of projecting and recognizing the subconscious. Everything is stuck and stale. We are not attracted to projections in art, relationships, career, or anything.

If blocking is an issue for you, you must look deeply at your whole self. You must not look for the quick fix or develop dependency on substances to bring you into momentary contact with the creative force. Such approaches are clearly destructive. It often seems that artists revel in self-destructive impulses that make it possible for them to temporarily contact the creative subconscious, and feel that this is what it means to be an artist. Such attitudes are born only of ignorance. Do not use your art as justification for self-destructiveness.

Eliminating inner blocking means you must devote time to a sincere program of inner exploration and emotional clearing. This is the same program that would be used for depression, which is likely to be present as well. As an artist, you have the advantage of already having a means at your disposal to help implement your quest: your art. Use your art consciously, whatever the art form, recognizing that it will draw from within you the subconscious, suppressed feelings that need to be cleared. As they come into awareness, be sure you are feeling them properly, not minimizing or mechanically "expressing" them in your work.

In her book, *The Artist's Way*, Julia Cameron discusses journaling, which she calls *morning pages*, as a means to unblocking. Allowing stream-of-consciousness to emerge on the page eventually reveals deeper feelings, desires, and suppressed contents of the subconscious, at which point they must be properly handled. These same principles may be applied to any art form - don't feel you must limit yourself to writing. Use them within your particular discipline, whether visual art, music, dance, or whatever.

Devote a certain period each day to scribbling in your media, without conscious censorship – practicing the NOW. Allow thoughts and feelings to enter the scribble. Practice handing over control to the higher intelligence. Create with "no-mind." Do not think, judge, or plan. Don't show the work to anyone. Use the practice simply to empty. This is a tremendous ritual for loosening up, building expressive ability, and opening the door for new original work – many of these scribbles will become part of finished pieces, as Cameron herself states regarding the morning pages she has written.

As you engage in this daily no-mind emptying, you may become aware of resistance to both the practice and to the emerging self. Honor the resistance. It is the blocking itself being revealed. Do not try to make it go away, do not condemn it, but do not yield to it either. It is part of yourself that is trying to act in your best interests, but is confused. Find a place for it, as if it is sitting at your side, present but not necessarily disabling you from working. As you welcome the resistance, accepting it and any momentary blocking that it might bring, you begin to make it possible for the resistance to change. As the resistance becomes honored, and even depicted in the art, it begins to soften. Begin with a portrayal of it and let it change by itself through moving to a process. Celebrate it, even create a ceremony around it if this appeals to you. Let the resistance speak. It will tell you about itself and why it believes it is acting in your best interests. As you befriend the resistance, it will eventually allow you to access the material it is protecting.

## burn-out

Burn-out occurs when we don't allow ourselves to recover and replenish the energy we expend in any activity. Simply understanding our human limits and being careful not to exceed them will enable us to avoid burning-out, and to engage art safely and sanely.

However, even though we understand this, we still allow ourselves to be driven to the point of burn-out, where we find ourselves incapable of functioning. When this happens, usually it is because we are misusing the art in some way – we are either compulsively seeking or avoiding, or both, through the art.

What do we seek? We seek fame, recognition, security, sex. Or perhaps we are not looking for such exciting things, but are only trying to find peace of mind, comfort, or healing through art. What do we avoid? Usually, the other side of what we are seeking: loneliness, fear, insignificance, worthlessness, and a range of other negative feelings.

Burn-out has become a way of life in our society, and before we know it we have fallen into it. We are so compulsive and addicted to anything that seems to offer any solace for our pain that we grab onto it and submerge ourselves in it. We run it into the ground, destroying all of its mystery and rendering it unable to provide the benefits it could.

As artists, it is easy for us to submerge ourselves in the art when the third stage hits – when we are let down, and feel critical and depressed, and when the subconscious negative takes on full significance. We retreat into the art so we can push those feelings out of awareness. We avoid handling them intelligently, and set the stage for burn-out.

Behind all burn-out is the avoidance of feeling. It's the motive for pushing ourselves so blindly. Just knowing this, and learning to approach feelings intelligently – to process them – is all we need to do to avoid the syndrome. As we release the tension due to those unresolved feelings, we no longer feel the impulse to escape through the art, and we are able to approach our art non-compulsively, genuinely attuned to it instead of abusing it.

## support

At times I thought I could be completely happy if I could just be with a woman who would love my music. She would lay on the floor in a dimly lit room in the evening, enraptured by me playing guitar and singing with passionate abandon, opening my heart to her, expressing all the feelings there – sorrow, joy, longing, love. All my yearnings for approval, sharing, and contact would be fulfilled.

But it was never to be. On the contrary, whenever I would play a piece of music for anyone, I didn't usually get any response that made me feel as if I had offered them something that might have been pleasing to them. It didn't matter if I had been working on a recording for days or weeks, totally moved by the intensity, soaring high in the second stage of the work. I would invite someone into my studio, roll the tape, and sit there dying, trying to appear to not need any kind of approving statement but knowing I wanted it. It felt like I was opening my soul, inviting them to share my deepest secrets, and the least they could do was offer some form of acknowledgment. When it didn't come I was hurt, and I had to try to disguise my hurt in order to appear not to seem juvenile about getting approval.

Although I suffered through this syndrome with many people, it was usually my intimate other that provided the strongest negative stimulus. It was in an eight year relationship in particular that I experienced this coldness for my music. Not that she was blatantly critical, she just never seemed to show interest. She was never there for the work. She never seemed to support me in my music by including it in her world, enjoying it, being proud of it, praising it and me, let alone reassuring me when I felt discouraged and needed a kind word. I put up with it because other parts of the relationship were satisfying – I thought I was in love – and I wasn't entirely conscious of what was going on between us anyway.

As the years passed and I kept getting deeper into psychological work, I started to acquire insights and vocabulary to identify patterns and dysfunctions. Naturally, I identified them first in her. She didn't have any heart. She lacked warmth. I had been fooled by her beauty, charm, and magnetism, mistaking them for deeper qualities of the soul such as supportiveness, caring, and the ability to nurture. This analysis appeared to be corroborated by her astrology chart, with Moon conjunct Saturn in the twelfth house, a sign of inability to be in touch with or express feelings in general. Later, I found out that my father had the same configuration.

But while there may have been some truth to this psychological appraisal, at some point I had to look at myself. I eventually realized I had attracted, and was attracted to, a person who was essentially mirroring the lack of supportiveness I extended to myself. In blaming her, I was missing the point. I saw that I needed to do in-depth work. If and when I was to clear the negativity within that had so enthusiastically attracted the mirror outside myself, things might change.

I understood that I needed to move into a new relationship with my unsupporting inner voice. First, to see fully what it was saying, which was a variation of the critical voice: I was untalented, I had no background in the arts or in music, my training was in another, unrelated field, I couldn't play guitar like many other people could, I couldn't write songs as well as some other people, my music productions were good, but there was something missing that prevented them from really making the grade. Endless fears and self-limiting feelings lurking in the background of my mind were brought forward into the light of awareness.

While some people might say these negative thoughts needed to be eradicated because they were attracting negative circumstances and people, I was aware of a deeper truth: That the power was held in the suppressed *feelings* behind the thoughts. That was what provided the energy for the attraction, and that energy could not be dispelled by simply turning away from associated thoughts or trying to change or recondition them. The way to proceed was to release the energy of the feelings by processing them – bringing them into consciousness, feeling them while maintaining a detached stance of acceptance, and witnessing them. This process of bringing consciousness to the negative feelings, of no longer pushing them out of awareness into the subconscious, would clear the negative suppressed energy, and the resultant self-limiting thoughts.

So what were the feelings behind the thoughts? As I sat with all those self-limiting thoughts, it didn't take long to come to a *feeling* of being worthless. It was a feeling of not being adequate – of being inadequate, incompetent. Working with this feeling over the course of a year led me to other times, including childhood experiences, when I perceived, probably subjectively and inaccurately, that I was being invalidated by others – teachers or peers. Large amounts of anger started to come to the surface. Working with the anger became a major focus for my processing work.

Going beyond the anger, I discovered the sense of inadequacy common to us all, although I may have had a larger share. Eventually, through the constant witnessing, I came to a place of transcendence of the feeling – no longer identified with it, seeing it from a more detached place. The feeling was also lessening and was not so much of a problem because I saw it more as a dualistic condition of life than as a personal issue: Inadequacy was just the other side of the feeling of being competent, and of getting recognition. Whenever the feeling of inadequacy again occurred, I was able to move beyond it, not by fighting it, but by welcoming it and making a place for it as a part of myself that needed to be nurtured.

I needed to provide support for myself from within. Expecting it to come from another was only setting me up for disappointment. Because my art was so important to me, it was hard to remain objective about this. I assumed that what I was doing was also important to others, or at least that they should recognize its importance for me and provide support as part of being a friend. But when we seek outside ourselves for that which we cannot provide from within, we do not find it.

Yet, in our humanness, we must acknowledge that we cannot avoid yearning for the support and approval of others. We must also accept this part of ourselves, and not try to bully ourselves into perfect independence. In this acceptance, we also accept the pain that comes when we do not find the support coming. Doing so, we naturally grow into a non-compulsive orientation towards outer support, being able to graciously enjoy it when it spontaneously arises.

# recognition

We live in an age of instant, electronic media, where it's possible to be taken from obscurity to world-wide fame overnight. It's an age where many people pay attention to a few; the few who are able to attract the fickle spotlight of the media; the few who become the superstars, in all areas of contemporary life. In the arts – whether film, music, literature, fine arts or any art – the superstar mentality has come to dominate. Films are financed and promoted largely because of box office appeal of the leading actors. In music, especially pop music, the focus is on a few commercially viable individuals. A few writers sell most of the fiction published. In painting, while generally reaching less people, the artists who are able to command significant sums for their work are part of a small, inner circle.

This situation is completely unique within the perspective of known history. Never has so much attention been directed towards so few. The implications are both good and bad. On the one hand, it is extraordinary that we have such access to excellence in art. The electronic age, along with the advent of the printing press, which historically happened just yesterday, has enabled us to be exposed to, to learn from, to become sophisticated about art to an extent previously undreamed of. If we desire, we can open our doors to the best musicians, painters, film-makers, or writers of the present or past and have them perform or exhibit in our living rooms. As artists, we can learn and be shaped by a wide variety of influences.

But what is the down side? It can be summed up in a few words: isolation, alienation, loneliness. These qualities have always been part of the human condition, but they appear to have become exacerbated today by the cultural, technological pressures to which we are exposed. The electronic age leaves us out of touch, in genuine ways, from each other. We turn to the TV or Internet for human contact; we read the paper; we talk to our therapists.

For artists, the impact is especially consequential. We think our art has no purpose, it is no good, it is not worth doing unless we are "successful," unless we have "made it" and become the object of the spotlight, a super-star. Yes, we can hang our paintings in the local coffee-house or sing our songs there; we can get our poem published in the local paper; we can have our own web-site, but does it satisfy us? Not usually. We have been brainwashed by our isolationist culture into thinking and feeling that we are not a success until we get some kind of mass exposure, which by definition is limited to an infinitesimal percentage of all producing artists. The system has evolved so that it is based on the tremendous frustration of those wanting to be seen, who never will be simply because of the logistics of media and other outlets. And even if we get the recognition, it usually does not give us what we want.

There is a legitimate need to share work. Even though I may create my work as part of a conscious process of self-discovery, I'm human, and I want to show someone else what I've done. I want to get a reaction – hopefully, an admiring one. I even might want to think that it might make a contribution to society in some way, that I might influence, help to heal, or teach what I've learned. These may be referred to as healthy ego-needs. They are to be honored and not denied, even though it is quite possible that as we grow our ego-needs will change in accordance with our changing perspective.

We start to run into trouble when we confuse healthy ego-needs with false neurotic needs. We buy into the super-star mentality, not really knowing it, and become driven by it. In selling out, we become market-oriented instead of soul-oriented; we think mainly in terms of how our art will appear to others. Our healthy ego-needs become confused and obscured.

A major premise of this book is that we can shift from being compulsively driven for recognition in our art by using it as a conscious path to the soul, to self-discovery, and to a sense of inner wholeness. This is what we really are seeking in our compulsive quest. When we shift our orientation and purpose, our compulsiveness will dissipate, our ego-needs will align with true needs and become such that perhaps we can be genuinely satisfied with simple recognition and a real connection to an intimate, interested, personal audience.

Moreover, art becomes meaningful. What a tragedy if art had no personal meaning unless we became an outward success. On the other hand, if the need for outward success is subjugated to the use of art as a personal pathway, it means that all artists can be successful, that success is not tied to any evaluation of objective talent.

The electronic age is an extension of the technology era. Just as technology resulted in dehumanization but contained a bright side as it impelled artists into unprecedented, individualistic, personal expression as a reaction, so too, the electronic age has swung so far to the side of isolation and major-media domination that it has inadvertently brought about its antithesis: Community is now being created because of isolation. Isolated and *fragmented*, we have had to actively seek out others with whom to relate. The result has been small, special interest, world-wide groupings that provide the new sense of community. This has largely taken place on the Internet, and although still not being optimal in promoting personal contact, either one-to-one or with an audience, it is at least an important avenue that will continue to expand.

For example, look at what's happening in popular music. There are innumerable sub-classifications of pop music, each attracting a certain audience. At this point in time, the whole music distribution system is in tremendous transition. Large record labels are no longer needed to market music. Musical artists are selling directly to the audience via the Internet. There's no reason this same kind of approach will not work in all of the arts.

The super-star mentality appears to have become a dinosaur. We have been conditioned to think that way but it is time to reverse that thinking. On the other hand, with fragmentation and direct marketing, it may be unlikely to sell huge quantities of our art, but do we need to? We will again become the small village – the global village – with its very own artists and troubadours who perform for their peers and are happy doing only that; an identity has been found that can satisfy healthy ego needs. And if something does come along that warrants mass attention, maybe it will happen.

Something is wrong with our thinking or the system or both if no satisfaction is to be found unless we become stars, or, perhaps less egotistically, unless someone else sees and appreciates our art, whatever form it takes. We are talented, sensitive people. As artists, we are dedicated and focused on a plane of being far above ordinary materialistic consciousness, a place of passion that gives meaning to life, a place that non-artists envy and admire. Is this not enough? Don't fall into the trap of thinking you need large-scale recognition to be happy.

So, how are we to get by?

First, make a priority of using your work as a means to personal growth. For me, it's to stay in the moment with my art; to surrender my yearning for recognition, recognizing that it will come on its own terms, on its own time, if it is to come at all, and that it is not the point of my art. The point is to continually refine – to perfect – my understanding and experience of creating art as a means of self-realization, which I can do even more effectively without the pressure of public notoriety and expectation. This is the higher aspect of creating art. This opportunity might not come again soon, and I want to take full advantage of it.

Second, make a priority of having a simple, reasonable outlet for your work. If we use our work only for growth and show it to no one, we are denying an important part of our humanness that needs to share and connect through the art – it's not *why* we're doing the art, but a *result* of having done it. Once we've centered ourselves in the experience of art as a means to the soul, we don't need as much recognition or approval to satisfy us, and low-profile self-marketing, exposure on the Internet, or the occasional exhibition is all we will need, and when we do manage to get our 15 minutes of fame, we will be unattached and delighted. If we are centered only on getting attention, we quickly become ambitious, ego-driven, and frustrated.

Another way to look at it is with the assistance of astrology, which tells us that there are cycles of development we go through relative to all aspects of our individuality. There are periods that are formative, in which we are developing and refining, or even in which we will have no interest in art, and there are periods when our personal technique will come together and be ready to show to the world. Knowing these cycles – either intuitively or through technical analysis of the birth chart – and accepting and relaxing into them is wise.

# 9

# The Loneliness Of The Artist

*Moving into soulfulness; Creating alone; Relationships;*
*Success; The Artist's path*

Loneliness can permeate the artistic lifestyle. In order to function as artists we need to be removed from the mainstream. We often feel out of place when surrounded by mass culture because we don't share those values. We need large amounts of time alone to do our work, or just to day-dream, to contact the muse, and before we know it, our aloneness turns to loneliness.

Often, the requirements for art attract those who are introverted and reclusive to begin with, and as they immerse themselves in its world, they begin a downward spiral into alienation and self-involvement. If we add this artistic loneliness to the existential loneliness we all suffer, we can arrive at a place where the experience of loneliness can become major.

Sometimes, it may seem that loneliness is necessary for art. It's hard to imagine van Gogh painting passionately in the fields all day and then coming home to a wife and kids. It's the pain that motivated him to produce the work. But must we resign ourselves to the pain, and our loneliness, in order to produce emotionally powerful art?

There is no doubt that strong feelings must be present for art to occur, and many times these feelings will be painful. But throughout this book we have been discussing how we may use art intelligently to explore, integrate, and heal these feelings. We do not want to be overcome by them, driven by them or become dependent upon them in order to create art, or use art as a means to suppress the feelings. Let's examine how this pertains to the problem of loneliness for the artist.

## creating alone

It is the nature of the art process, as we covered in chapter seven, to culminate in coming down from the art high into the low of the third step, where loneliness can prevail. Even the high itself, with its tremendous joy, occurs in solitude. Our elation in the creative act, what we live for, is very closely followed by its shadow, loneliness.

This has always been my experience. All my creative highs, in which I feel emotionally moved and transported to another realm have always occurred by myself, in my studio. Along with the ecstasy comes a sorrow that I have no one with me with whom to share it – the feelings seem to almost come together. And if I try to share it later with other people, it's never the same. I'm unable to take them to that place that is so important to me, that I want so much to show them.

The loneliness that comes up in the third stage of art is tied to our existential experience of loneliness – it's part of what it means to be human in this present stage of our evolution. Existential loneliness is inherent within the process of individuation. We break our identification with our parents at a certain age; the result is a feeling of freedom and independence, but it can be accompanied by loneliness. Similarly, we break our identifications with many other forms of support that we need as we grow, but eventually must outgrow. Each time we leave something behind, we experience loneliness. Our sense of individuality is dualistically balanced by the sense of loneliness. When we do art, we accelerate the awareness of this loneliness.

We must recognize this condition as one of opportunity. As artists, we are spiritual travelers. We are moving fast, faster than most. In our journey, we're bound to run into the negative – that is our job – but sometimes we forget that this negative will manifest within us as feelings, and as loneliness. It may be said that as we work with our loneliness and integrate it, we perform this task for the collective, perhaps even carrying this feeling to a certain extent for the rest of us. We are the emotional trailblazers, preparing others and beginning the immense task of integrating loneliness.

## loneliness as archetype

That the archetype of the artist can include loneliness has been a recurring theme in literature, but in modern times this concept has not been depicted with more tenderness or wisdom than in an episode from the exceptional TV series *thirty-something*.

While most of the characters in the *thirty-something* ensemble are artistic, only Melissa has the courage, talent, or other psychological make-up necessary to commit to a career as an artist, as a photographer. But she's also the only one who never seems to find a lasting relationship. She wants it desperately, and wants children, but there's something about her, portrayed brilliantly by Melanie Mayron, that has this aura of singleness, and of loneliness, of being doomed to a succession of failed love affairs in spite of her spunkiness, humor, and good-heartedness.

The culmination of this syndrome takes place in a beautifully written and directed episode in which she has a gallery showing of her photographs. The show represents a peak achievement for her, something she has been working towards. It happens that the show itself is a very personal statement about her relationships, a pictorial record of all the men who have been her lovers. In a sense, perhaps somewhat unconsciously, she has been working with the theme of her loneliness, trying to integrate it through contemplation of the sensitive portraits she has taken of them, which also poignantly reveal herself behind the camera – the way she sees them, her need for them, and the pathos of their impermanence.

A sub-plot that has been developing is an encounter she has with an old acquaintance she has not seen since grade school, when he had an unrequited crush on her. As they meet now, she is pleasantly surprised to feel an attraction for him, and invites him to the opening. Her unconscious expectation is that he will fill the void, the show will be a success and he will be there with her to share it.

However, when he arrives, he's with another woman. There's been a misunderstanding between them if not an outright act of revenge on his part for the pain she caused him in the past, or maybe it's just her karma coming back to her. Melissa is distraught, and runs to the rest-room to barricade herself from the realization that she will always be alone. The success of the gallery opening is only a mockery. It means nothing, and worse, it is implying that in order to have the success, she must pay for it by giving up any hope for intimacy.

At that point her good friend Ellen, who is usually flustered and spacey, comes into the bathroom to rescue her with an incredibly compassionate display of just being present for her in her anguish – it's one of the most powerful scenes in the whole series. Melissa pulls herself together, and moves to a place of acceptance. She goes back to the crowd and is genuinely able to enjoy the attention, praise, and love they shower on her. She circulates through the room, radiant and beaming.

## artists in relationship

Many of us today, not only artists, are without intimate partners. Present society is in a tumultuous stage regarding its reassessment of male/female roles and the nature of relationship. We tend to no longer put up with what we regard as any kind of emotional incompatibility or abuse, or with a relationship based on mundane or economic considerations. In our liberation, we are more aware of our needs, more in tune with our souls, and know what we want in a partner. We want a meeting on all levels, a spiritual and emotional as well as physical melding, and we hold out until we find it. But unfortunately, this holding out can turn into a permanent state of affairs. It can seem as though we will never find someone, and we can begin to spend more and more time at our art in the absence of intimate contact. This *channeling* of heart into art has ramifications that need to be looked at. An interesting perspective for doing this is suggested by the esoteric science of astrology.

In astrology, both art and love are ruled by the same planet, Venus. This means the same basic type of psychic energy – the energy of the heart chakra – is used in both. We therefore have the choice of whether we will use our limited amount of Venus energy for art or relationship; possibly an archaic Newtonian view, but one I have found to hold up in practice. If we are not able or choose not to spend the energy in a love relationship, we can spend it in the creation of art. The energy finds an outlet, and does not become stale and stagnated.

Moreover, in order to produce art with strong emotional impact, the Venus energy of the heart must become fully engaged, passionately. The passion that we stir and focus into the art, that brings life to the art, is a large part of the reason why the experience of making art is so emotionally stimulating and fulfilling. In bringing life to the art, we become alive, we function on a plane of being unknown to the average person. It's the reason we have no interest in much of what interests the rest of the world – the chase for possessions or power.

But the down side to this is that if we choose to passionately engage in art, as we must to produce any personally significant work, we can limit our potential for loving relationship. If we are in a relationship, it is easy for it to start to suffer. Our partner may become jealous of the time we spend at our work and the peak emotional experiences we are having with it and not them, especially if they do not have any passionate interest in their life, art or otherwise, and expect to find emotional fulfillment solely from the relationship. As a result, they may begin to undermine the work, perhaps unconsciously, subtly criticizing it and withholding the support we would like to get from them.

If we are not in a relationship, we suffer a different kind of stress. Art becomes our lover, and we look to it to satisfy the deep thirst of the soul. We become dependent on art. In turning to art as a means to the heart, we do have experiences that are satisfying, but they never fully take the place of a relationship. Intimate relationship appears to be a basic, intuitive, human need, and I would look suspiciously at anyone who says they have dispensed with the need or completely sublimated it through work or spiritual practice, as well as art. Perhaps for periods we may take part in a spiritual monastic lifestyle, or become the monk-artist, but in the end, it seems we will come back to this need.

If intimacy is a genuine need, and we don't have it but try to satisfy it through our art, where does that leave us? Even though we may be able to find a degree of satisfaction, perhaps a large and significant degree, in our art, behind it will be the sense of lack of relationship – loneliness. This lack is not to be covered over by the creative art act. Trying to do so – trying to satisfy all our Venus needs through the art – is where we get into trouble. We end by suppressing the need, not satisfying it.

So our stance, if we are in a relationship, will be to become conscious that we need to divide our Venus energy between our art and our partner; that our partner may have a legitimate objection if we do not reserve any of ourselves for them, which can easily happen when we become immersed in the work. Or at the least, perhaps it can be discussed that we need certain periods to put ourselves completely into our work, and it does not mean we do not care about them.

If we are not in relationship, and are experiencing loneliness as a result, our stance will be one of putting ourselves completely into our work during the periods we devote to work, but also remaining aware of our loneliness, sitting with it, processing it, perhaps including it in the art if it happens spontaneously as Melissa seems to have done. We don't fall into the trap of substituting art for human contact. We remain open to the possibilities of contact, and responsive if it occurs. We trust that we are being guided and that our experience is developing in us what needs to be developed.

Actually, we are not in a much different place than if we had a relationship. The trap we fall into in a relationship is thinking that it will satisfy our loneliness. Our expectations burden the relationship and often this pressure and the demands that result are central in destroying the relationship. A key to maintaining intimate relationship is not expecting it will ultimately solve our loneliness problem, because it won't. We may experience short-term relief at the start, but when it eventually falters, we are again back with our loneliness, and start blaming the relationship. Even in a relationship, therefore, we must allow for loneliness.

Loneliness is part of the human condition. It may drive us to seek relationship, but will not be ultimately satisfied through the relationship. It must be integrated, by taking it through the steps of processing; accepting and experiencing, even celebrating it. Through the process, we will eventually find where it is leading us.

## success and loneliness

Take a hard look at what drives you in the unrelenting quest for recognition. Isn't the need to satisfy loneliness a major part of it? We fall into the trap of thinking we will fill the emptiness by connecting to others through the art. Or perhaps they will admire us and want us because of our artistic achievements.

Often, when we become compulsive about doing art, when we spend all our time focused on it, when we don't have any other contact with the outside world, the art becomes the sole means for us to make that contact. We fixate on the art – perhaps unconsciously – clinging to it to make us feel part of something larger than ourselves, that we are connecting to other people, another person.

If we "succeed" in this quest, we find ourselves in the same position as many other celebrities in the arts and entertainment world. We trade the possibility of intimate contact with another person for intimacy with our audience, but it doesn't work. We are never to be fulfilled, and perhaps too late, when opportunities for real intimacy are lost, we realize our mistake. As Jeanne Moreau said, "Success means nothing; you can't make love to it."

We become an apparent outward success, adored by millions, yet unfulfilled and lonely on the inside, and even more acutely lonely in proportion to the degree of adoration received. Is there any doubt that this is what propels celebrities into despondency and substance abuse? In her biography, Janis Joplin was said to turn to alcohol or drugs *after* her performance, not before as one might think. Jackson Pollack's success only increased his dissatisfaction, loneliness, and propensity for drink, which killed him. It's the feelings *after* that are so difficult, after you've given yourself and gotten back the recognition from the audience, that you feel the loneliness.

We all seek recognition to try to satisfy the deep emptiness and loneliness inside, and we all feel the backlash. We may get some recognition, and it may appear to satisfy us for the moment, but then the depression sets in, worse than before, with a vengeance. It's telling us we are misusing our art. We cannot seek to avoid the loneliness, we must face it directly and process it.

## the artist's path

If there is to be so much loneliness for the artist, why do we continue? In many ways, we continue to make art because we have no choice. It is our nature, our *dharma*, our role in the cosmic drama. We know it is right for us at our present stage on the path. We see that it does connect us to deeper, lost parts of ourselves. It gives us contact with the essence of life, with energies and emotions usually hidden below the surface that alone make life seem worthwhile after we have had a sampling of them.

We understand, even though our understanding may be incomplete and partially based on faith, that these moments of rapture are to be balanced in our dualistic world by some kind of compensating dark experience. If we move to a place of acceptance of that darkness as it takes the form of loneliness, we are moving forward into eventual integration, transcendence and growth as a person and an artist.

Don't be driven by loneliness. Loneliness and related feelings of emptiness and dissatisfaction are the basic spiritual problem that we hope to resolve with all our compulsive striving and attachment to relationships, sex, recognition, career, and security symbols.

Rather than impetuously chasing after such illusive goals, simply sit with your loneliness. Let it become a central part of your spiritual and artistic practice if it is a current problem. Just being with the feeling, gently accepting it, will eventually change you and your experience of it.

# 10

# Art And Sex

*Integrating sexuality with the art path;*
*Wholeness; The creative force;*
*Re-directing; Homosexuality*

Our life experience is based on a *dualistic* manifestation of spirit into matter. In its most basic form, the dualism is known to us as the archetypal energies of male and female, yin and yang, positive and negative. Before manifest creation, when these two energies were united, there was no tension between them. In separation, a restless tension has come into being. The two forces instinctually attract each other in the longing to merge, to be re-united, and for the bliss and peace of wholeness.

## the quest for wholeness through sex

Sex, our most powerful emotion, is the expression of that longing for wholeness, or oneness. In the sexual act, we temporarily but intensely regain the wholeness of the divided male and female. In the sexual relationship, we establish an ongoing link that offsets our existential feelings of isolation and incompleteness. As sex blends with love, we enter an arena of the highest potential for human fulfillment. Our ecstasy can be sublime. But, as we all know, devastation can be only steps behind. Because, whether we approach the sexual experience as transient and physical or as a loving and committed relationship, it will never serve to ultimately give us the essential wholeness that we seek in it; dependence on it to do so results in collapse. We must find wholeness within, not outside ourselves, through the integration of the dualistic inner self, especially the inner male and female. When achieved, the inner integration will allow a stable relationship to manifest on the physical plane. But if we seek the relationship first, as the means to wholeness, we will not succeed. This is one of the important lessons we are to learn. In the meantime, the search for oneness through sex makes the world, as we know it, go around.

It has been said that the passion for sex is really the passion for God. But what is God? For me, realization of the subconscious - especially its *superconsciousness* aspect - is identical to the realization of God. And the path of recognizing, reclaiming, and integrating lost parts of ourselves, as we have explored relative to art throughout this book, leads directly to the wholeness that we seek through sex. As we move more and more into this wholeness, we find that we are less driven by the compulsive need to merge through sex. The shifting of perspective changes gradually as we grow. We do not need to force any such change. Forcing is not possible anyway, and will probably lead to results counter to our intentions.

The movement towards wholeness within includes the merging of the inner male and female. The inner male and female take form in countless dualistic qualities and aspects of ourselves. The dualism appears to us as a pairing of opposites. One of the pair of opposites usually attracts us; the other usually repels us and is likely to be buried in the subconscious through our rejection of it. In reconciling the opposites through uncovering the suppressed part and integrating it, we directly integrate the inner male and female. Proceeding with this self-realization process, we bring more and more of the inner male and female together. We experience the fulfillment that we seek in the primary, unconscious urge for wholeness and the sexual impulse that results from it.

# the creative force

In addition to providing the temporary but powerful experience of oneness, sex is the basic creative act; two come together to make new life. We might conclude that sexual energy is inherently creative, and that its re-direction to other areas of life can result in different forms of creativity. This is the basis for the theory of *transmutation* of sexual energy that has appeared in schools of psychology. It has been observed that sexual energy can be channeled into other forms of expression, including the arts. I generally agree with this, except to make a slight clarification: I do not believe it is sexual energy that is inherently creative; I believe it is energy itself that is creative. When I speak of energy, I am referring to the hidden, psychic force that permeates all life to which yogis refer as *prana*.

Prana itself is the creative life force. It possesses intelligence, which it demonstrates in healing and balancing the human organism on all levels. The energy itself may be experienced, or expressed into consciousness, through any of the chakras. The chakras are clearing-houses that direct the energy to the various departments of life. When the energy is directed through the sexual chakra, activity is felt there, and the creative result is new life. When the energy is directed through other chakras, creativity of completely different types is brought forth. This is important to understand so you don't fall into the mistake of thinking that the creative force itself has sexual overtones; or that art must contain sex; or that you are being especially creative if your work contains sexual feelings or thoughts. Sexual feelings, of course, are a vital part of our emotional makeup, and must be included in any comprehensive portrait of the human condition, but the raw creative force itself is not sexual. It may manifest in myriad ways.

In our culture, we are undergoing a general obsessive-compulsiveness about sex that has resulted from previous centuries of repression. Add to this the ordinarily intense interest that humans have in the subject, and we come to a place where we have developed a strong addiction, as may be observed in our entertainment media and advertising. As in any addiction, we think we can satisfy our craving with more of the substance, but the cravings do not go away, even with excessive indulgence, and we become confused and despondent.

Normally, we unconsciously condemn ourselves for having the compulsive feelings, and healing is thwarted. But we must see that sexual compulsiveness is just another part of ourselves to be accepted, without acting it out. There is nothing fundamentally wrong with it, even though it indicates a condition of imbalance. When we process the compulsiveness, accepting and feeling it without acting it out, we begin the healing. We become aware of deeper core feelings and begin to work with them.

The core feelings may be of emptiness, loneliness, separation, futility, loss; in fact, any feeling may be behind any addictive compulsion, depending on the individual. Men appear to be particularly vulnerable to sexual addiction because it has been observed that they try to work off feelings and tension in general through sex more than women. Lately, however, perhaps as a result of the evolving women's movement and their reclaiming of the inner male, it's been my impression that women are also falling into the snare of trying to work off feelings through sex instead of through genuine process, although a certain amount of this is probably good in order to bring the repressed maleness into balance.

Many of us approach art with a background of sexual compulsiveness. It's possible the art will then contain sexual or romantic themes, which is growth-enhancing if the art explores them with awareness and detachment, and does not simply become masturbatory. If this happens, the art does not serve to enlighten; it merely serves as a vehicle for a continuing self-engulfment.

## re-directing

It has been said that sex can free our creative energies. Contrarily, it has been said that sex will drain our creative energies. We have probably experienced both of these statements to be true.

If we are relatively non-compulsive about sex, and have been sexually frustrated, a fulfilling sexual encounter can be liberating; it seems as if our creativity has been held down by our frustration. Especially in the early stages of a new relationship, we find ourselves abundantly creative. It might be concluded that sex and/or love is important to maintain our capacity to produce art. There is nothing wrong with enjoying this state whenever it comes about. However, we usually find that the creative bursts we experience as a result of sex are temporary, and that reliance upon sex in order to produce art only contributes to sexual compulsiveness and dependency. Sex becomes another drug needed to contact the muse. Moreover, the attitude that our sexual (or other) needs must be fulfilled before we can create is disempowering. We know that some of our best work is done when we are deep in pain. Among other things, the pain serves to break down the crystallization that prevents us from opening to the new; and sexual deprivation would certainly qualify as a source of pain.

On the other hand, there is a vast body of esoteric tradition that holds that other "higher" centers become activated and creative when energy is sublimated from the sexual. In fact, it is assumed by esoteric teachers that real yoga does not begin until the sexual force is re-directed. My personal experience agrees with this. Because so much of our energy is compulsively, or instinctively, directed into the sexual chakra, the re-direction, or re-channeling into the "higher" chakras results in greater capacity for creativity and consciousness. When this happens, the diminishment of sexual activity is not felt as a regretful loss, as we may be inclined to imagine. Instead, we find that the blossoming of the higher centers actually brings a more evolved and fulfilling sense of life. And it does not mean we leave sex behind; we only put aside the compulsiveness that has been tormenting us.

To rechannel sexual energy, some kind of program may be adopted for limited or extended periods of time, from a few months to a few years or indefinitely, depending on your inclinations. The simplest implementation of re-directing, usually found in spiritual and monastic orders, is a ban on all sexual activity, either with or without a partner – celibacy. However, if handled incorrectly, celibacy can and usually does, in my opinion, result in repression and undesirable repercussions. Even though advocated with spiritual goals in mind, and tenderly explained and understood, the ban encourages the unconscious *rejection* of the sexual force.

The attitude of rejection is counter to the principles of enlightened self-work. We begin to see sex as a negative part of ourselves. On the contrary, we need to move to a place of *acceptance* of ourselves, on all levels. Our basic problem is that we are immersed in self-rejection, especially on the emotional level. Often, we continue the rejection of negative emotions for spiritual reasons; we think this is how to become spiritual. Instead, all perceived negative emotions must be accepted, experienced, and processed to completion, *but not acted upon*, so we can reclaim those suppressed parts of ourselves. It is the same with sex. We need to accept the sexual feeling, but must train ourselves not to act on it and, instead, to move it to the higher centers. This subtle shifting of attitude makes for a significant difference in our experience.

In yoga, there are techniques – especially important are the basic hatha yoga postures – that serve to condition the body, mind, and emotions for the safe transmutation of the sexual force, and allow celibacy to be approached intelligently. It is not enough to simply turn away from sex. This will lead to health backlash problems such as the high incidence of prostate cancer among Catholic priests and emotional difficulties such as edginess and instability. The energy must not be allowed to build up and stagnate in the sexual chakra; the energetic channels in the physical and psychic bodies must be opened so that the energy is really moving to the higher centers. Breath and body techniques are essential, along with the proper attitude of acceptance. Techniques for transmutation have perhaps been developed to their pinnacle in the *Tantra* and particularly *Taoist* traditions, in which loving sex is engaged in, but without conventional orgasm. Orgasm, for both men and women, is experienced inwardly in the entire body, moving the energy to the higher centers.

You may not care to take re-direction to such extremes, but knowing about it may influence your attitude about your sexual needs. As you enter into art, you are naturally practicing redirection. You may experience a loss of sexual interest as you put all your energy into the work. When the work is completed, or when taking a break, the sexual impulse returns. Such ability to channel the inner energy represents a non-compulsive, balanced condition. Our art serves as a vehicle for our spiritual growth, even if we are imperfect in relation to it and bring a certain compulsiveness to it or engage in a certain amount of escapism through it. In the passion that we bring to our art – our eagerness to be involved in it, the demands it makes for our complete soul, the joy and the pain we experience through it – we employ perhaps the best means to channel our energy to a higher level of expression and consciousness.

## art and homosexuality

A discussion of art and sex would not be complete without an acknowledgment of the presence of homosexuality in the arts. Homosexuality is only just beginning to come into the light in our historical era, and there still exists an incomplete understanding, and even fear of it. Certainly most academics or clinical psychologists don't have the foggiest notion of what it's about – they generally have regarded it as an aberration, an arrestment of psychological growth, that must be corrected. Institutions such as the Catholic church still simply condemn it, encouraging guilt and repression in many who may still be struggling with their self-definition.

This misguided and ignorant viewpoint of the mainstream, which may be shifting now as a result of the radical consciousness-raising in human rights that has taken place over the last forty years, has contributed greatly to the anguished soul-searching that many gays go through to find themselves – to reach a point of adjustment and final self-acceptance. Self-acceptance is the key here, because no amount of trying to change will ever have any effect.

A few years ago I happened to see for the first time *Night and Day*, a film made in 1946 about the life of Cole Porter, starring Cary Grant. Cole Porter is one of my all-time heroes. As a young songwriter, I spent hours at the piano, sheet music in front of me, totally entranced by the magical, haunting blend of melody, harmony, and catchy, romantic, pop lyrics in songs such as *I've Got You Under My Skin, What Is This Thing Called Love, In The Still Of The Night, Night and Day*, and many others he wrote in the twenties and thirties.

Although I enjoyed hearing all the songs as I watched the film, something about it didn't seem right. I checked into a more truthful biography about Cole and was irked to discover that most of the biographical material in the film was fiction. One of the most important discrepancies was that he was portrayed as a man torn between career and a passionate marriage, with the career winning. In reality, while he was married, the marriage was only for appearances. Cole was completely gay and active in the lifestyle right from his college years at Yale, the biography states. The revelation was a mild shock to me. As a straight man, my subjective vision had not pictured him that way, even though another part of me had suspected that, yep, here's a male artist who's enormously talented, suave, and sophisticated – he must be gay.

Recently, there's been the remake of Cole's story, now called *Delovely*, with Kevin Kline as the lead. I was interested in seeing the film, curious if his homosexuality would be included this time. It was, but again, I was disappointed in the way it was handled. He was portrayed as being able to form only superficial, glittery sexual relationships with men, with his deeper emotional needs and attachments directed toward his wife. While this could be possible, it seems like a distortion and even an insult; homosexuality is again portrayed as an aberration, a limitation, a problem. There's no acknowledgment that a mature gay relationship of course includes emotional attachment and deep love just as a straight relationship may.

But to get back to our concern, why are so many artists gay? Furthermore, is it necessary to be gay to be a great artist? Sometimes it seems that way. In order to answer these questions, we must explore the nature of art from another angle, and how that relates to the homosexual orientation.

Art is a product of the feminine. Connecting and opening to the heart – the basic capacity for feeling – are feminine traits. Women, therefore, are *generally* more naturally suited for the arts than men. Women are closer to the heart, closer to feelings, express feelings more easily. Men, *generally*, are not focused on feelings, but on getting things done – taking time for feelings only gets in the way.

Furthermore, any artist may be feminine or masculine in their approach to art. A feminine writer's work will often resemble a personal journal, a record and experience of feelings. A masculine writer will produce an action novel. A feminine songwriter will be singing about important inner experiences; a masculine musician will be composing anti-establishment punk rock anthems. The important point here is that when I refer to masculine or feminine, I am not talking about physical gender. I am referring to inner psychological characteristics, which sometimes have no relation to the physical body. Thus, it's possible to have a dominant, inner psychological orientation opposite to the body type, and this is what is known as homosexuality.

A gay man often has feminine-dominant inner psychological characteristics, and a gay woman often has masculine-dominant inner psychological characteristics. Not that this always has to be the case – there are gay men and women who do not appear to have a dominant, reverse, inner sexual-psychological orientation. However, we would not expect a gay man without a strong inner female to excel as an artist, because it is the strong inner female – in anyone – that gives the artistic capacity.

Nobody knows for sure why homosexuality exists. Certainly I am not an expert, and my intent here is to only help foster acceptance and to bring light to it relative to the arts in any way I can. There are probably varying psychological reasons that account for it, and every case would have to be considered individually. Nor do I necessarily feel that "reasons" for it need to be found. Sometimes we think we need to "understand" something before we can accept it, but this is only another limiting left-brain concept. Acceptance does not need understanding, and if necessary, understanding will come at the right time, on its own, after acceptance has worked on us.

However, that being said, I would like to share an intuitive insight I've had about the homosexual orientation that I have found quite interesting, and may be of interest to some, especially those with a metaphysical disposition. Since having had this insight several years ago, I have come across two other reputable occult writers (Cyril Scott, Betty Bethards) who have proposed the same idea. These two writers asserted that it applied to all cases; I might be more inclined to suggest that it may only be one of the possible explanations.

As we reincarnate from life to life, we usually maintain the same sex for a number of subsequent lifetimes. But then, when we are ready to change sexes, primarily to experience psychological attributes that are relatively inaccessible in our current sex, it may not always be possible to make a complete transition, and we change only halfway. A homosexual lifetime is the incarnation between changing sexes – an incomplete transition. A woman changing into a man will acquire a masculine body, but still be predominantly feminine inside. A man becoming a woman will acquire the body, but still be predominantly masculine inwardly. In their next incarnations, they will fully make the switch. If this theory is true, most of us at some point will likely undergo a homosexual lifetime. It is not to be considered that the experience represents any kind of deficiency.

We could further theorize that it may not always be necessary to undergo a homosexual incarnation when changing sexes if there was already a developed sense of the opposite sex psychological attributes. Then, the shift would not be so difficult; but since this is not common, most of us will need to experience the transitionary state. It is also possible that the experience may be deliberately chosen – perhaps repeatedly – by a soul as an essential part of its growth, such as to awaken compassion, to pay off karma, or to provide certain advantages that will help achieve the goals of the incarnation.

One of these goals may be to excel as an artist. When we survey the artists who have been recognized as masters throughout the centuries as well as today, it appears that many if not most of them are homosexual. Apparently, being homosexual conveys ability in the arts. And while I will try to be as non-sexist as possible, it also appears that the majority of these artists, for whatever reason, have been men. Although there may have been sociological reasons that the women's movement has been addressing about why women have not been widely recognized as artists, it does not logically follow that gay women would be expected to excel in the arts, since their inner orientation is masculine; we would expect them to be drawn to masculine types of activity. Of course, these are broad generalizations, and there will always be exceptions. Just as a straight man may be an exceptional artist, so may a gay woman. This is because we all possess the psychological characteristics of both sexes inside. The straight man who is a good artist must possess a well-developed female psychological side; the same with a gay woman, even though in both the inner masculine is dominant.

This aligns with the overall goal of *androgyny* that is another way of looking at soul development – developing, balancing, being able to access and express both inner sexual qualities, male and female, yang and yin. However, when both inner sexual qualities are functioning, it is important that one or the other dominate. This establishes an identity required to function psychologically in our dualistic world. Even though there may be a well-developed balance of sexual inner qualities, in a hetero orientation, same sex inner attributes are dominant, while in a homosexual orientation, opposite sex inner qualities are dominant.

When people first start to work on developing the inner sexual qualities that may have been latent, they often fall into the trap of going too far, shifting their personality artificially, letting their minds dictate how they should be instead of stilling the mind and observing what is truly inside. Thus, hetero men become unnaturally effeminate, and hetero women become unnaturally masculine – often trying to compete with men on men's terms – leading to inner confusion. Similarly, homosexual men trying to be macho and homosexual women trying to be girlie are simply distorting the reality that they were born with and must affirm.

But why can a gay man possess extraordinary artistic talent? We could speculate that having a male body confers abilities inherent to the male archetype that are helpful for the materialization of feeling in form; manipulation of the material world is what males are good at. Other male qualities necessary for success may also be accessed such as ego-drive, ambition, determination, physical strength, and, in the past, more possibilities for recognition. In the end, we don't know for sure. We just know the way things are. But we do know that if you are a gay man, or woman, the important thing you must do is first move to a complete place of acceptance regarding your psychological / sexual make-up. In today's world, with the tremendous focus on gay consciousness, it appears that most gays have done this.

# 11

# Post-Modern Art

*A contemporary vision of art and society;*
*The quest for truth*

*Presence* has become an important element in the Post-Modern art world, starting in the eighties. Before that, Western art was different. Although there had existed for twenty years or so the Conceptual/Minimalist schools, which tended to remove emotion from the art piece, there still largely existed what has come to be called the *Modernist* esthetic, existing for the preceding hundred or so years, coinciding with the advent of the Industrial Age. Modernism was founded on idealism, optimism, the portrayal of good versus evil with good winning, belief in the value of "beauty," belief that things can be brought together, that the human condition can be improved, and that we can work towards these goals.

It was a romantic esthetic, reflected by the growing theme of romantic fulfillment in popular music. However, disillusionment in the Modernist esthetic began early in the first half of the Twentieth Century with the cataclysmic horrors of global war. The belief in a utopian futuristic vision became untenable to artists at the forefront of contemporary culture, and *Post-Modernism* finally came into full force, coinciding with a post-industrial, or Electronic Age.

The Post-Modern esthetic was not nihilistic, however, but remarkably life-affirming. Rather than believing in a future when things will be made right, or gloomily resigning itself to misery, the Post-Modern stance leaped to the holistic conclusion that everything is all right *now*; we don't need to change anything, we don't even need new things, all we need is to realize the truth that we are whole – that to be whole means to embrace all aspects of existence, both so-called good and bad. In seeking to propagate the transcendental vision of unity and realization of the existing harmonious network of life, Post-Modern art relied upon recycling art of the past. The juxtaposition and choice of the art of the past was key in determining the impact of the art. Thus, artists *appropriated* other artist's work in their own, architecture incorporated classical design elements, music shifted beyond the romantic fixation, both in contemporary classical and pop, and recycled old musical bits, recently having become known as *sampling*.

It was assumed that all that needed to be done in the Post-Modern art experience was to see the old in a new way. In order to *see*, you had to put aside already learned concepts that have remained active in the mind, preventing clear vision. The mind has to be stilled; perception – the perception of *what is* – is to be cultivated. When the mind is stilled, the experience of *witnessing* automatically takes place – it's the sense of watching dispassionately in a detached way; the sense of not being identified with the object of attention, of being something different from it. Witnessing is essentially the same as presence. In presence, we witness, we see, we experience *what is*. As with Squat Theater, presence was incorporated into performance as an essential element, both in the performer to activate the performance, and as a requirement for the viewer to fully appreciate it.

It's amazing to me that all these precepts formed within a sociologically-based art movement and not within a primarily spiritually-based movement, because they are the foundation of mystical experience and practice. Of course, Eastern philosophies were widely known at the time, within the exact same circles that were concerned with artistic problems. It is no surprise that they must have significantly influenced thinking, but it is still of wonder that the movement was taken to such a popular level, peaking in the eighties.

Many people at the time may not have been aware of the philosophy behind the movement but still were influenced by it, including myself. I remember being strongly attracted to the sensibility of the new art – it had a refreshing, liberating quality about it. My particular art form then was singing/songwriting. I played primarily acoustic guitar. My influences had been the folk and rock movement of the late sixties and seventies. The way I experienced the shift was in terms of emotional emphasis. The old music was "heart-centered," while the new art was centered somewhere else – it seemed beyond the heart, still including it, but in a more enlightened way.

Most Modernist western art, including classical music, from which contemporary pop music has been derived, is based on this traditional heart-centered orientation. The work is "emotional," it tells a story, its intent is to portray and arouse emotions in the viewer. Think of Beethoven. In a way, this kind of art is *product art* – portraying the known. This kind of approach to art can be important, especially to one who may need to come into closer contact with the emotions. However, there is also a certain kind of identification and engulfment with the heart that precludes the condition of witnessing, and ultimately, gets in the way of optimal healing. While we want to include the emotional component in our art, we are more interested in setting the stage for *process art*, where subconscious feeling will be revealed through its projection. We are not primarily interested in portraying feelings in the art that we already know.

In emotional healing, one of the requirements is to step beyond the feeling, to let it be, to not try to change it but to accept it as part of a whole – just as in the Post-Modern philosophy – to witness it, and experience it. In this process, the suppressed emotional charge that has been locked in the body is released and balance occurs. If we take sides, and believe that we must attain the "positive" feeling and escape from the "negative" feeling, we prevent healing and are likely to become addicted to the positive. This is, unfortunately, often the case with those new or ill-informed on the New Age path. True healing and evolution of consciousness occur only through acceptance of our total emotional selves, not the rejection of painful parts of ourselves, even in the name of healing.

The heart center corresponds to the heart chakra, the home of many of our most important emotions, including love, belonging, romance, but also hate, loneliness, and rejection. If we are engulfed in the heart, we tend to believe we need to attain the positive feelings of the heart; we write songs or novels about finding true love; we paint pretty pictures of sunsets and children; we sculpt the erotic ideal of our dreams; we compose, or listen to, moving symphonies that churn and carry our feelings up and down. We remain enmeshed, engulfed in the heart, never to truly find satisfaction because we deny the reality of the heart, which is that emotional experience is dualistic, both pleasurable and painful.

When we move beyond the heart to the place of the witness, we move to the third eye chakra, the traditional seat of consciousness located on the forehead. Here, we shift our identity and consciousness to the witness. It does not mean we deny what is going on in the heart, only that we are no longer engulfed in it. We have found a detached perspective that is essential to the healing in the heart. Art that takes place from this center does not necessarily need to tell a story. It will often have no goal because goals presume the desirability of getting to a place better than where we are now, which is seen to be a misguided presumption. It will often seek to convey a feeling of "trance" through repetition of key elements, especially in music. But it also will be concerned with feelings. As you might imagine, *Pig Child Fire* brought up tremendous feelings for me and I believe the rest of the audience. But we were also free to project our own feelings onto the performance more than if there was a well-defined story line. And because it was all presented with powerfully restrained presence – witnessing – it catalyzed the audience into that same metaphysical space.

The art consciousness of the Post-Modern movement has pointed us in this direction. Today, we see a conglomerate of types of art. We see much heart-centered art along with what might be called neo post-modern, and we have the option of choosing the style of art that we may personally need. It is entirely possible to engage in heart-centered art with consciousness and presence, in the witness. As we move into the witness, in presence, we begin the process of healing in art.

## the quest for truth

I'd like to conclude this book with a look at one of the most important artists of the Post-Modern period, Salvador Dali. I find Dali to be an inspiring figure for many reasons, but primarily because he exemplifies a tremendous spirit in using art as a pathway to self-discovery and self-realization. He shows that such a pathway is compatible with producing art that can be viable and successful in the marketplace, and can come to be considered "great" art. Dali's approach to art incorporates many of the principles we have been discussing.

Dali may be considered to be one of the first Post-Modernists. Much of his important work was done in the 1920 – 1930's, influenced by the world wars and scientific mood of that time. Dali's specific type of painting was linked with the *Surrealist* movement; he has become famous for his images of melting clocks, even though his total output covers a vast range of subject matter and a few different major styles.

Dali and the Surrealists were much influenced by Freud, who was a current public figure, expounding his new theory of the subconscious. The Surrealists, excited by this intellectual and spiritual frontier, were dedicated to bringing the subconscious to light through art. The Surrealist axiom was that uncovering the subconscious was only of value if undertaken with utter honesty; there must be no watering-down of what has been discovered to fit in with moral, societal, or even esthetic values. The goal was to uncover the psychological shadow, with all its mystery and repressed pain.

Freud's book *The Interpretation of Dreams* further impressed the Surrealists profoundly with its premise that the subconscious could be known through dreams. Surrealism became essentially the portrayal of symbolic dream imagery, accounting for its bizarre images that twist and blend into each other. Dali's melting clocks were a comment on the different nature of time on the dreamscape, or the astral plane, indicating he had first-hand experience with this level of being. His writings also reveal a ravenous inquisitiveness and inventiveness about theories of perception and altered states that took him into the mystical. He devised private ceremonies and rituals that would access deep right-brained realms of the soul, awakening and expanding his artistic sensibilities.

In his art, we at once see the radical shift from most previous art of that time, with its Victorian overtones, to the exploration of the inner and personal. Dali has been said to be the finest exponent of Surrealism, and in keeping with the Freudian emphasis, much of his imagery is of the repressed sexual, where he demonstrates great courage. Can you imagine exhibiting a painting called *The Great Masturbator* in post-Victorian Europe? Not many of us would have the courage to show such a work even today. The painting is autobiographical; its theme directly reflects highly personal issues Dali was dealing with – his difficulty with normal sexual intimacy, his retreat into self-eroticism, and his feelings of guilt, remorse, and incapacitation from abusing his energy.

Of course, Dali was also the flamboyant showman, and much of his courage leaned into audacity. We must not overlook that he carefully calculated the shock value of his work; but still, beyond this, there is a clear sense of honesty permeating the work – that the work would not hold up regardless of the showmanship without this honesty, and that the honesty is an important factor that draws us to it. His range of work and the degree to which he was able to bring his personal self into it are awesome and inspiring. Virtually everything that happened to him went into the art, both conscious experience and dreamscape elements combining to create the unearthly, other-worldly ambiance that made him famous.

For example, his relationship with his parents often entered his work. His father was alienated by Dali's early themes, and essentially disowned him. This was quite painful to Dali, although he refused to change the work, and the remoteness of his father appears in many of his paintings, sometimes as a cold aloof figure, sometimes more obscurely portrayed. Dali felt his mother was responsible for his sexual aberrations, and his ambivalence towards her is often a focus, alongside themes of romantic idealization and despondency. The romantic idealizations were centered on his wife, Gala, with whom Dali had a devoted fifty year relationship. She was his model, she represented his salvation, and he has said he wouldn't have been able to function without her. Of course, this sounds like dependency and may not necessarily have been the healthiest of relationships; Dali is obviously projecting his positive suppressed feminine onto her, and the counter-balancing negative onto other female targets, such as in *The Specter of Sex-Appeal*, a sarcastic image of a decrepit, rotting female body.

Dali's drawing ability and esthetic sense are absolutely masterful, and the degree to which he is able to combine brilliantly-executed representational elements with brilliantly-conceived fantasy elements had much to do with his success. Moreover, in his unrelenting quest for new perspectives, he foresaw major art movements in op art, photo-realism, dual image (where small images interact to form larger images) and others. Dali's work in general is symbolic and figurative; nowhere does he launch into abstract expression, and his later period even returns to a more classical feeling. The symbolic nature of the work directly ties into the Freudian approach to the subconscious. "Symbols," whether appearing in dreams or reality, were the means by which the subconscious was seen to represent itself. Thus, we see throughout Dali's work a tendency to the product-portrayal mode.

But in the formation of these compositions, we can see him moving into a process mode. He portrays these symbols in preliminary sketches, letting them interact with each other, and as a painting evolves, new symbols are evoked. The sense we get is that he is portraying these soul elements as they come forth without necessarily trying to decipher them; he does not ultimately know what they mean, and he is at peace with this; he lets them retain their mystery, allowing that this process itself might lead eventually to an integration, a coming together, a transcendence of these aspects of himself. He has been quoted, "If you know what the painting means, you might as well not make it."

As powerful as his work was in opening the doors to his personal as well as the collective psyche and setting a revolutionary example for the world to follow, from our current perspective we can see where it might have gone next to make the inquiry even more rewarding. Even though there is the dramatic portrayal of intensely personal themes in the work, we get a sense of "distancing" from feelings instead of engaging them as might be found more in abstract process art, where feelings may be thought to be more fully *embodied* in the art instead of only being symbolized by it. Most of his paintings, as bizarre as they are, have a studied, planned, distanced sense about them, and we know he did preliminary layouts for many paintings, developing them.

This tendency to symbolize and not engage fully was exactly in line with the psychological (Freudian) thought of the times. Resolution of psychological trauma was thought to come from analysis of the subconscious, through the symbols it presented. Analyzing these symbols was the means to "understand" what they meant. It was assumed that to understand how any "complex" had originated was enough to "cure" it. As psychological thought evolved, it was realized that this is not enough, and that there must be an emphasis on actively releasing suppressed feelings of the subconscious shadow – getting into and working on the feeling level – for psychological healing. Psychology then moved to a stance of "expression," assuming that to release feelings, they must be expressed and not held in.

Today, as I have explained in this and my other works, we are on the forefront of another psychological revolution. We understand that feelings must be released, but that it is not expression that accomplishes this. Instead, the feelings must be integrated – rejoined and reconnected, brought back from their split-off place to a place of wholeness – through genuine acceptance and experience of them. Using art as a means to enter this experiencing deeply is what this book has been about.

As I think back through the pages I have written, I can't help but question if I have really been able to convey what it means to experience a feeling – what it means to stop the mental processes, to shift into another psychic mode, to sense a presence with the emotional energetic in a way that we are normally unaware of. But then, I reassure myself. I know that once pointed in the right direction, you will discover these things – and other things – for yourself. Really, all you need to be told is to look within.

I wish you the very best in your art quest. I know it will become a life-long source of fulfillment and sustenance for you.

## about John Ruskan the artist

John has been on the artist's path all of his life. Working primarily in the music field, he has composed and recorded over 10 albums throughout the years, and continues to release new work. He feels that working as an artist has been a critical factor in his personal growth, especially regarding emotional maturing. He was the owner of Crossfire Recording, one of the first 'budget' recording studios in New York City in the artistically vibrant 1980's, which hosted a great number of spirited independent recording projects. He started out as a singer-songwriter, playing guitar and performing solo in public. As electronic music synthesizers became available, he was strongly attracted to the uniqueness of their sound, and started producing compositions ranging from abstract, free-form music to pop song-based pieces. One of John's guiding artistic principles was always to bring together seemingly opposite forms into a new, hybrid expression. Thus, the singer-songwriter merged with the electronic and resulted in New Wave Rock. Another life-long passion has always been consciousness study and Yoga. This merged with the music and produced meditative, instrumental albums unique in the New Age music field, aimed at evoking the deep subconscious along with the transcendental witness. Throughout, John has been completely comfortable playing all the parts of any musical composition, which was possible because of technological breakthroughs in multi-track recording and synthesizers. He has come to feel more like a painter than a musician, composing and executing the entire musical landscape, and this natural solo artist inclination has enabled him to more easily use his art as a tool for consciousness work, as he has written about here.

In recent years, John's main career focus has been in the psychology field, turning his life-long avocation in consciousness work into a vocation, and re-inventing himself as a psychologist and writer. A companion book to this present one, called *Moon Walking*, presents a spectrum of stark and startling right-brained vignettes, straight from the personal and collective subconscious. His previous book, which brought together yet another set of opposites, East and West psychology with a new original synthesis called *Emotional Clearing*, has been widely hailed by experts. His music and other writing is available at **www.johnruskan.com**. His ongoing Emotional Clearing work is at **www.emclear.com**.

other works by John:

## Emotional Clearing:
### Releasing Negative Feelings and Awakening Unconditional Happiness (book)

Enlightenment is not possible without resolving subconscious negative emotions and karmic patterns. *Emotional Clearing* is a true East/West cutting-edge inner process. It may be applied as a self-therapy or with the energetic support of a therapist in private session. Entering a meditative alpha-state, you gently transform undesirable trapped feelings, and compensating compulsive behaviors and corresponding limiting life circumstances evaporate.

## Moon Walking:
### An Excursion Into Emotion And Art (book)

In this radically unique and evocative work, John Ruskan takes the reader on a journey into the collective unconscious archetypal world of feeling. He blends fiction and fantasy with East/West psychology to help awaken forgotten emotional parts of ourselves that must be brought into the light as a vital step to personal evolution and healing.

## Burning Karma:
### Honoring Adversity In Order To Exhaust Negative Inner Energies
### (double music CD)

DISC I *The Struggle* is a song-based, provocative, consciousness-raising dramatization of the challenges, doubts, and pitfalls that may be encountered on the inward journey.

DISC II *The Transcendence* consists of soft instrumental ambient pieces that will support and comfort you as you make the shift into higher consciousness.

# https://johnruskan.com

# https://emclear.com

Made in United States
Orlando, FL
16 May 2022

17933591R00124